FELL'S BEGINNER'S GUIDE TO

BRIDGE

FOR ALL AGES

FELL'S BEGINNER'S GUIDE TO

B R I D G E

FOR ALL AGES

by Lucille Place

CARTOONS BY ROBERT G. STRONG

ABOUT THE AUTHOR BY CHARLES C. KING, M.D.

A World of Books That Fill a Need

FREDERICK FELL PUBLISHERS, INC.   NEW YORK

Library of Congress Cataloging in Publication Data

Place, Lucille.
  Fell's beginner's guide to bridge for all ages.

  Published in 1959 under title: Beginning bridge
for all ages.
  SUMMARY: An introduction to the rules and strategy
of bridge designed for the player "who first has to
learn the difference between a Spade and a Club."
  1. Contract bridge. [1. Bridge (Game)]
I. Strong, Robert G. II. Title. III. Title:
Bridge for all ages.
GV1282.3.P56 1975   795.4'15   75-13971
ISBN 0-88391-043-8

For information address:
Frederick Fell Publishers, Inc.
386 Park Avenue South
New York, N. Y. 10016

Published simultaneously in Canada by
George J. McLeod, Limited, Toronto 2B, Ontario

Manufactured in the United States of America

"A Queen and One"

To Terry Jean

My future teen-age bridge player

ACKNOWLEDGMENTS

I want to express my thanks and appreciation to the American Bridge Teachers' Association, and especially to George S. Gooden, bridge teacher and author of Carmel, California, for their inspirational ideas that I received at our Convention in Dallas. I would also like to express my thanks to Boyd R. Hughes of Columbia, S.C., for allowing me to use his "Call The Director" rule book.

Table of Contents

[8]

Preface

I have written this material for the individual who first has to learn the difference between a Spade and a Club. Many adults as well as teen-agers fall into this category. I have found that age has nothing to do with whether you can learn to play bridge. The interest you have and the desire to learn are the main ingredients necessary. Learning to play bridge is like building a house; you have to take one step at a time, and if you haven't built a firm foundation, your house will not be well built. Many bridge players have played for years without first having had this foundation, and consequently it is difficult for them to communicate intelligently with their partners. They know how to open a bid and respond the first time, but after that they are bidding by "ear."

I am sure that you have heard the remark: "I will never learn to play bridge." Many beginners have felt this way because there are so many rules to remember in the bidding. So often, if you understand why a rule is made or can associate the rule with something with which you are familiar, you can remember it better. For this reason I am using the "association method" of teaching as much as possible so that you won't have to do so much memorizing. I also feel that you could never be a good bridge player if you played from a memory chart. Since there are thousands of ways that bridge hands can be dealt, you must be able to play by using your own reasoning ability rather than from just memorizing a bunch of rules. Some of my associations may seem rather elementary, but by being such I hope you will retain them longer.

One of my methods of simplifying bridge is to place the Point Count in groups. You will learn to *Bid, Respond,* and *Rebid* in each

[13]

group. As you read this book, you may observe that I am occasionally sacrificing a point in order to keep the bidding in these groups. I have done this deliberately so as not to confuse the player who first has to learn the difference between a Club and a Spade. To those of you who are not experts, up until the past couple of years when the points were changed, they were as I have them in my book. I feel that the changes complicate things just a little for the beginner, and the changes in Point Count are so minor that your game will not be impaired by the 1-point difference where it occurs.

In writing this material I have found that my own two teen-agers have been my best advisers. Jimmy, fifteen years of age (who is my duplicate bridge partner occasionally) and Charmian, twelve (who is my severest critic), have helped me write this book so that boys and girls and adult beginners may use it more effectively.

I want to thank Mrs. J. Walter Cobb, Headmistress of Lausanne School for Girls, Col. Ross Lynn, Headmaster of Memphis University School for Boys, and all of the boys and girls who have helped me prove that bridge can be a very wholesome and educational recreation for teen-agers. Having instructed students from six to eighteen years of age in the above institutions and in my home classes, I have found that bridge teaches them to think, and to be thoughtful of others, to have self-confidence and many other admirable qualities. With the younger boys and girls it serves as an "ice breaker" when they are shy in new situations. Since it is an entirely new field for them, they feel that they have to be experts before they can play. Their problem is solved, however, after the first few hands, because they realize that their fellow teen-agers aren't experts either.

In Memphis, many of our young girls are having bridge luncheons, the boys and girls are playing bridge at the swimming pools, in the country clubs and at evening socials. They have found that bridge is a very healthy part of their social life, and as we all know, the social life of our youth is one of the most important phases of growing up. I hope that by giving them, as well as adults, a bridge textbook that they can understand, bridge can become the challenge to them that it is to many of us.

In my adult classes I have found that the student who has no knowledge of bridge falls into the same category as the Junior High student. I have used this material just as effectively with this group as I have with the teen-agers. Since an active bridge player must have an active mind, I feel that bridge is one of the very best preventives of "growing old."

There is one thing that I want my students to learn at the first lesson: Your partner has as much right to be there as you. Always treat him as you would want to be treated. When you become such a good bridge player that you never make a mistake, then you will have the right to be critical of your partner.

My bridge philosophy: "If you leave the game with more friends than you had when you came, you are declared the winner."

LUCILLE PLACE

CHAPTER I

The Mechanics of the Game of Bridge

Bridge is a game played with a deck of 52 cards. The deck is divided into four suits: 13 Spades, 13 Hearts, 13 Diamonds, and 13 Clubs. The following cards are in each suit: Ace, King, Queen, Jack, 10, 9, 8, 7, 6, 5, 4, 3, and 2. The A K Q J 10 are called honor cards. The rest are called spot cards.

Spades and Hearts are called Major Suits. Diamonds and Clubs are called Minor Suits. These suits also have ranks:

> Spades (highest)
>
> Hearts
>
> Diamonds
>
> Clubs (lowest)

THE DRAW

TO SELECT PARTNERS AND THE DEALER

Bridge is played with four players. The 52 cards are spread out in the center of the card table, face down. Each player selects a card. The two players selecting the highest cards are *Partners*, and the two selecting the lowest cards are *Partners*. The player selecting the highest card of all is the *Dealer*.

Suppose *all* players *select* a 9 spot? The players selecting the 9 of Spades and the 9 of Hearts are *Partners*. The players selecting the 9 of

Diamonds and the 9 of Clubs are *Partners*. The player who selects the highest ranking suit, the 9 of Spades, is the *Dealer*.

We will call our players North, East, South and West. Since partners always sit opposite each other, we will have a North and South team, and an East and West team.

THE SHUFFLE

The opponent to the left of the Dealer shuffles the cards for the new Dealer. After the first shuffle the partner of the Dealer will shuffle a second deck of cards during the deal. He places the cards to his right so that his right hand opponent can deal next.

THE CUT

The Dealer places the deck of cards in front of his right hand opponent who divides the deck into two parts, placing the top part toward the Dealer. The Dealer then picks up the cards farthest from him and places them on top of the first part. The cards must be cut at least four cards down or more than four cards up from the bottom.

THE DEALER

The Dealer distributes the cards clockwise around the table, one at a time face down, starting with the player at his left and ending with himself. (Each player will have 13 cards.)

There are two parts to bridge:

1. Bidding.

2. Playing the hand.

1. *Bidding.* The dealer always starts the bidding process. His first call, however, can be a pass. At this point, we are concerned only with

the mechanics of bidding. You will learn the how's and why's later. Let's assume the bidding went like this:

South is the Dealer and bids first.

South	West	North	East
1 Heart	*Pass*	*1 Spade*	*Pass*
2 Spades	*Pass*	*Pass*	*Pass*

Observe the following:

(a) The last bid was *2 Spades,* so this is the final contract and Spades are *Trumps.**

(b) North bid the Spade suit *first,* so the contract is his. He plays the hand and is called the *Declarer.*

(c) There were three passes before the bidding stopped.

2. *Playing the Hand*

From the above example, two things are decided: (a) The final contract is *2 Spades.* (b) North is the *Declarer* and plays the hand.

Let's discuss this further.

(a) The *Final Contract*

This means North and South have made an oral contract to take a certain number of *Tricks.*** Since they stopped the bid at the level of two, North, who is the *Declarer,* must take eight out of the possible thirteen tricks. First he must take a

---

* *Trumps*—The last suit mentioned in the bidding is *always* trumps, and this suit has certain power over other suits. In explaining a *Trick* (see footnote below) we say that the highest card played takes the trick. If one of the players is out of a suit, he may put a trump card on it and the trick is his no matter how small the trump is.

** *Trick*—A card is led or put on the table by one player. Each player, in turn, follows with a card in that suit if he has one. The player putting down the highest card (in the suit led) gets all four cards. This is called a *Trick.* If a player puts down a 2 of Diamonds and all other players are out of Diamonds but put down high cards of other suits, the first player takes the trick because Diamonds were led. You must follow suit when you can.

[19]

Book. This is always the first six tricks that he takes. After the *Book*, he starts counting tricks to see if he has made his bid.

(b) North plays the hand.

I mentioned earlier that the play who first names the suit which is determined as the trumps always plays the hand and is called the *Declarer*. The partner of the *Declarer* is called the *Dummy*. After the *Declarer's* left hand opponent leads out a card which is called the *Opening Lead, then* (and only then) the *Dummy* lays his cards in front of him on the table. The cards are arranged according to suits, with the trump suit on the Dummy's right. *Declarer plays both his hand and Dummy's hand in their proper turn.* Dummy speaks no more until the next hand is dealt. (See Chapter XV on Laws.) The object of the game is scoring points. (See Chapter XIV on Scoring.)

CHAPTER II

Opening 1 Bids with 13 to 21 Points

BIDDING

Bidding is merely an accepted way of telling your partner the kind of cards that you have in your hand. In the Morse Code, when a receiver hears three dots and a dash, he knows this means the letter "V." When a bridge player hears his partner say, *"One Spade,"* he knows his partner has at least four Spades and 13 points in his hand. In our bridge "communicating system," if you know how to send a message to your partner, he must know how to interpret this message and send you an answer. These messages can say, "Partner, slow down or we're going to be in trouble," or "Partner, I have a good hand; keep on bidding." They can also say, "Partner, proceed with caution. I'm not sure." Before the telegraph operator can be successful, he must first learn the Morse Code. Before the bridge player can be successful, he must learn the "Bridge Code."

When you first look at the 13 cards that have been dealt to you, you see a certain number of "hidden points." In order to open the bidding, you must have as many points in your hand as you have cards. So you must have 13. Why can't we associate our first "group" of points with the ages of our Junior High boys and girls? They are the 13, 14 and 15 year olds. They remind me of the minimum hands. They are old enough to start getting around town but not old enough to go very far. Keeping this in mind, I shall "group" the other hands:

13, 14 and 15 points—Junior High hands.

16, 17 and 18 points—High School hands.

19, 20 and sometimes 21 points—College hands.

22 points or more (sometimes 21)—Grownup hands.

You will not be concerned about grouping your hand as the opening bidder until you start *Rebidding*.

Have you ever noticed how brave a six-year-old becomes when he has joined hands with a thirteen-year-old? This reminds me of the second bidder on our team, who is called the *Responder*. After the thirteen-year-old can *Open the Bidding*, then he and the six-year-old can join "bridge hands" to make a bid. This gives us our "grouping" for the *Responder*.

RESPONDER'S GROUPINGS

6, 7, 8 and 9 points—Primary hands.

10, 11 and 12 points—Intermediate hands. (These hands are beginning to grow up a little.)

13, 14 and 15 points—Junior High hands.

16, 17 and 18 points—High School hands.

19 points or more—*Responder's* Grownup hands.

In some places the legal adult age is 18. So we will assume that in our *Responder's* bridge world he is also grown up at 18. So any hand with *more than 18 points* (19) is a *Grownup hand*.

POINT COUNT

How to find your "hidden points"

There are two ways to find "hidden points" in your hand:

1. High-Card points.

2. Distributional points.

1. High-Card Points

   Each Ace counts 4 points.

   Each King counts 3 points.

   Each Queen counts 2 points.

   Each Jack counts 1 point.

2. Distributional Points

   After you have arranged your hand according to suits, you may find one or more of the following *three situations: Voids, Singletons, and Doubletons*. It is from these three situations that you find your "hidden" *Distributional Points*.

   A *Void* (no cards in a suit) counts 3 points.

   A *Singleton* (one card in a suit) counts 2 points.

   A *Doubleton* (two cards in a suit) counts 1 point.

   Why do short suits make your hands more valuable? Let's suppose you have a void in Hearts and you have several Spade trumps. If your opponent leads the Ace of Hearts, is the trick his? No, because you are void in Hearts and will play a trump on his Ace.

You must add your "high-card" points to your "distributional" points to determine the number of points that you have in your hand.

26 POINTS + 8-CARD TRUMP SUIT = 10 TRICKS

Before a bridge partnership can intelligently bid a game of 4 Hearts or 4 Spades, which is a ten-trick contract, they must communicate and establish the fact that they have 26 hidden points between the partnership, plus an eight-card suit which they will name as trumps. *26 points plus high cards in all four suits will also produce a game of 3 No Trump.* However, it will take 29 points to make a game of 5 Diamonds or 5 Clubs.

33 POINTS + 8-CARD TRUMP SUIT + 3 ACES = LITTLE SLAM

37 POINTS + 8-CARD TRUMP SUIT + 4 ACES AND 3 KINGS = GRAND SLAM

[23]

33 points plus 3 Aces will normally produce a Little Slam, which is a bid of six, and 37 points plus all four Aces and all three Kings will produce a Grand Slam, which is a bid of seven.

QUICK TRICKS

Besides needing 13 points to open a bid, you must promise your partner 2 *Quick Tricks*. (This is for a possible future defensive bid.) A *Quick Trick* is a card that will take a trick either the first or second time a suit is played, i.e., the A K will take two tricks. K Q will take one trick because if the King loses to the Ace on the first round, the Queen can take the next trick. If you have the A K Q, you have only 2 Quick Tricks because your Quick Tricks have to be taken on the first two rounds, not the third. In a defensive play, your Queen will probably be trumped.

QUICK TRICK TABLE

2 Quick Tricks	1½ Quick Tricks	1 Quick Trick	½ Quick Trick
A K	A Q	A or K Q	K x

OPENING BID OF 1 OF A SUIT

Your Junior High (13, 14 and 15 point hands), High School (16, 17 and 18 point hands), and your College (19, 20 and sometimes 21 point hands) are all *opened* with a *1 Bid*.

When you get a *Grownup* hand (22 points or more—sometimes 21), you *start thinking* about your *Opening 2 Bids*. (See Chapter IX on "Opening 2 Bids" and Chapter VIII on "No Trump Bids.")

Up to now, you have learned that you must have 13 points and 2 *Quick Tricks* to open a bid. The last and most important requirement is that you *must* have a *Rebid*. Until you become more familiar with the game of bridge, let's work with the hand that has a *Rebiddable* five-card suit, i.e., Q J x x x or better. Not all hands will have a five-card suit. Some will have only a four-card suit, or maybe two or three four-card suits.

Note: A four-card suit cannot be *Rebid* unless your partner has raised it. See Chapter VII on "Which Suit to Bid First."

[24]

QUIZ

In the following hands, *count your points, Quick Tricks, group your hand* and *give your bid*. (In all hands, an x means any card smaller than a 10.)

(1) ♠ K x x x   ♡ A J x x x   ◇ K Q x   ♣ A
Points_____ Quick Tricks_____ Group_____ Your bid_____

(2) ♠ A J x   ♡ K Q x x x   ◇ x x x   ♣ A x
Points_____ Quick Tricks_____ Group_____ Your bid_____

(3) ♠ A K x x x   ♡ A x x   ◇ K x   ♣ K x x
Points_____ Quick Tricks_____ Group_____ Your bid_____

(4) ♠ A Q x   ♡ A x x x x   ◇ K x x x   ♣ x
Points_____ Quick Tricks_____ Group_____ Your bid_____

(5) ♠ A K x x x   ♡ x x x   ◇ K x x   ♣ x x
Points_____ Quick Tricks_____ Group_____ Your bid_____

(6) ♠ Q J x x x   ♡ K Q x   ◇ A   ♣ x x x x
Points_____ Quick Tricks_____ Group_____ Your bid_____

(7) ♠ A K x   ♡ Q J x   ◇ x x   ♣ A K Q x x
Points_____ Quick Tricks_____ Group_____ Your bid_____

(8) ♠ A K x   ♡ A K x x x   ◇ J x x   ♣ x x
Points_____ Quick Tricks_____ Group_____ Your bid_____

(9) ♠ A x x   ♡ K Q x x x   ◇ x x   ♣ x x x
Points_____ Quick Tricks_____ Group_____ Your bid_____

(10) ♠ x x   ♡ K Q J x x x   ◇ A x x   ♣ K x
Points_____ Quick Tricks_____ Group_____ Your bid_____

(11) ♠ K Q x   ♡ A K J x x   ◇ x x x   ♣ x x
Points_____ Quick Tricks_____ Group_____ Your bid_____

(12) ♠ A x x   ♡ A K x x x   ◇ Q x x   ♣ x x
Points_____ Quick Tricks_____ Group_____ Your bid_____

(13) ♠ K x x x   ♡ A J x x x   ◇ K Q x   ♣ x
Points_____ Quick Tricks_____ Group_____ Your bid_____

(14) ♠ A K x x x   ♡ J x x   ◇ K   ♣ K x x x
Points_____ Quick Tricks_____ Group_____ Your bid_____

(15)   ♠ A J x   ♡ K Q x x x   ◊ x x x   ♣ A K
       Points_____ Quick Tricks_____ Group_____ Your bid_____

(16)   ♠ x x x   ♡ Q J x   ◊ x x   ♣ A K Q x x
       Points_____ Quick Tricks_____ Group_____ Your bid_____

ANSWERS

(1)   19 points, 3½ Quick Tricks, College hand, bid 1 Heart.

(2)   15 points, 3 Quick Tricks, Junior High hand, bid 1 Heart.

(3)   18 points, 4 Quick Tricks, High School hand, bid 1 Spade.

(4)   15 points, 3 Quick Tricks, Junior High hand, bid 1 Heart.

(5)   11 points, 2½ Quick Tricks, Intermediate hand, pass (can't open).

(6)   14 points, 2 Quick Tricks, Junior High hand, bid 1 Spade.

(7)   20 points, 4 Quick Tricks, College hand, bid 1 Club.

(8)   16 points, 4 Quick Tricks, High School hand, bid 1 Heart.

(9)   10 points, 2 Quick Tricks, Intermediate hand, pass (can't open).

(10)   15 points, 2½ Quick Tricks, Junior High hand, bid 1 Heart.

(11)   14 points, 3 Quick Tricks, Junior High hand, bid 1 Heart.

(12)   14 points, 3 Quick Tricks, Junior High hand, bid 1 Heart.

(13)   15 points, 2½ Quick Tricks, Junior High hand, bid 1 Heart.

(14)   15 points, 2½ Quick Tricks, Junior High hand, bid 1 Spade.
(Since the King of Diamonds is unguarded, you must deduct 1 point, giving the King 2 points, and add 2 for the singleton)*

(15)   18 points, 4 Quick Tricks, High School hand, bid 1 Heart.

(16)   13 points, 2 Quick Tricks, Junior High hand, bid 1 Club.

---

* *Note:* A guarded honor is an honor card that has with it enough cards of the same suit to protect it from being taken by a higher card, i.e., a King has to have one other card to fall on the Ace. A Queen has

to have two other cards to fall on the Ace and King. A Jack has to have three other cards to fall on the Ace, King, and Queen.

When an honor is involved in a distributional situation such as a King singleton, a Q x doubleton, etc., you will notice that the honor is unguarded and you must deduct 1 point from the high-card value before you add distributional points such as in the above hand. The King singleton is unguarded so the King will get only 2 points; then add 2 points for the singleton, making the King singleton count 4 points. When a Jack is involved, since it received only 1 point to begin with, now it is considered just as if it were an x card. When you have J x x, however, you will notice that the Jack is still unguarded, *but* it is not involved in a distribution situation such as singleton or doubleton. In this situation, the Jack will receive its usual 1-point value.

A KING MUST HAVE ONE TO GUARD IT.

CHAPTER III

Responder's 6, 7, 8 and 9 Point Primary Hands

Before *Rebids by the Opening Bidder* can be intelligently discussed, you must first be able to interpret the message given you by the *Responder*.

Since the *Responder* has to assume that you opened the bidding with only 13 points (until you rebid and tell him more), all *Responses* will be to the 13, 14 or 15 point Junior High hands.

The Primary boys and girls are limited in their activities just as the 6, 7, 8 and 9 point hands are limited. These hands can only bid once unless they are pushed. (See "Rebids by the Responder with 6, 7, 8 or 9 Points.") There are *only* three messages this group can send:

1. *Raise your partner's suit.* This is an instance where the Point Count was changed to vary 1 point. I am sacrificing this point for simplicity.)

2. *Bid 1 No Trump*.

3. *Bid 1 over 1*, i.e., *Opener* bids 1 Heart, *Responder* bids 1 Spade.

EXAMPLES

1. *Raise your partner's suit.*

As South you hold

♠ J x x   ♡ K x x   ♢ Q x x x x   ♣ x x

The bidding:

North *Opens 1 Heart*. South *Responds 2 Hearts* (7 points).

A QUEEN NEEDS TWO PROTECTING CARDS.

Message:

"Partner, I have 6, 7, 8 or 9 points and adequate trump support."

Adequate Trump Support is the following cards (or better) in the suit bid by your partner. An honor card with two small cards or four small cards:

A x x   K x x   Q x x   J x x or x x x x

The first question that you will want to ask yourself after your partner makes a bid is, "Am I able to raise my partner's suit?" If so, no matter how strong your hand is, or what your bid will be, you should re-evaluate your hand in two ways:

(a) Distribution

Usual distributional points:	When raising Partner:
Voids—3 points	Voids—5 points
Singletons—2 points	Singletons—3 points
Doubletons—1 point	Doubletons—1 point

(b) Promoting Honors

If you have adequate trump support containing honors, give 1 extra point for the honors *unless* they already add up to 4 points, i.e., with A x x or K J x, do not add a point because the honors already count 4 points. With J x x, Q x x, K x x, or Q J x, add 1 extra point because they do not add up to 4 points.

When to Deduct Points

(1) Although an honor and two small cards are adequate trump support, you must deduct a point for having *only* three trumps. Why? Because your partner's suit may be a four-card suit.

(2) Deduct 1 point for having a square hand. (No voids, singletons, or doubletons.)

2. *Bid 1 No Trump* (Artificial No Trump). This means that your partnership does not have to have guarded honors in all four suits.

As South you hold

♠ J x x   ♡ x x x   ◇ Q x x x   ♣ K x x

The bidding:

> North *Opens 1 Heart.* South *Responds 1 No Trump* (6 points).

> We stated earlier that suits have ranks. Spades are highest, Hearts next, then Diamonds and Clubs. The No Trump is the highest-ranking bid of all. If a player bids 1 Club, another player bids 1 No Trump, then any suit bid by the next player has to be at the two level because they are all lower in rank.

Message:

"Partner, I have 6, 7, 8 or 9 points, but do not have adequate trump support and I cannot bid a suit of my own at a one level, so I'm just keeping the bidding open with my 6 to 9 points. You must remember, however, that my 6 to 9 points are in high cards."

Note: If the contract is played at No Trump, it simply means that no suit is trumps. The highest card in the suit that is led takes the trick.

3.   *Bid 1 over 1.* (This means a bid of 1 over a bid of 1, i.e., 1 Heart—1 Spade, showing 6 to 18 points.

As South you hold

♠ A J x x x   ♡ x x   ◇ K x x   ♣ x x x

The bidding:

> North *Opens 1 Heart.* South *Responds 1 Spade* (9 points. If you have a suit of your own to bid, then you count partner's doubleton 1 point for distribution).

Message:

"Partner, I have 6, 7, 8 or 9 points, *but* I could also have up to 18 points. *You must bid again* so I will have a chance to tell you on my *Rebid* whether I have a Primary hand or a stronger hand."

Note: To *rebid* as 1 over 1 with only 6, 7, 8 or 9 points, you have only one bid unless "pushed," or "showing a preference." (See "Rebid

by the Responder with 6, 7, 8 or 9 Points," page 55.) With 10, 11 or 12 points, you have two convenient bids. With 13 to 15 points, see that a game is reached in a major suit or No Trump. With 16 to 18 points, see that a game is reached in some contract.

QUIZ

In the following hands, you are the *Responder*, your partner is the *Opening Bidder*. East and West pass in all situations.

Hand #1   ♠ x x x   ♡ J x x x   ◇ K x x x x   ♣ x

a. Partner opens with *1 Spade*
   Your points_____ Group_____ Your *Response*_____?

b. Partner opens with *1 Diamond*
   Your points_____ Group_____ Your *Response*_____?

c. Partner opens with *1 Heart*
   Your points_____ Group_____ Your *Response*_____?

d. Partner opens with *1 Club*
   Your points_____ Group_____ Your *Response*_____?

ANSWERS

Hand #1

a. 6 points. Primary. *Pass.* You can't raise your partner because you don't have adequate trump support. You can't bid *1 No Trump* because your 6 points are not in high cards, so you must pass.

b. 8 points. Primary. *Bid 2 Diamonds.* Since you were able to support partner's suit you will give the King of Diamonds 4 points and promote the singleton to 3 points instead of 2. The raise in partner's suit limits your hand to 6, 7, 8 or 9 points.

c. 8 points. Primary. *Bid 2 Hearts.* Same rule as above.

d. 4 points. Pre-School. *Pass.* When your singleton is in the suit partner has bid and you don't have a suit of your own to bid, you don't count it as a distributional point. (You can't trump in on your partner's trump suit, can you?)

Hand #2   ♠ x x   ♡ K x x   ◇ J x x x   ♣ Q x x x

a. Partner opens with *1 Club*
   Your points_____ Group_____ Your *Response*_____?

b. Partner opens with *1 Heart*
   Your points_____ Group_____ Your *Response*_____?

c. Partner opens with *1 Diamond*
   Your points_____ Group_____ Your *Response*_____?

d. Partner opens with *1 Spade*
   Your points_____ Group_____ Your *Response*_____?

ANSWERS

Hand #2

a. 8 points. Primary. *Bid 2 Clubs*. Since you can support partner's Club suit, you promote the Queen of Clubs to 3 points.

b. 7 points. Primary. *Bid 2 Hearts*. Since you can support partner's suit, you must promote the King of Hearts to 4 points, but you have to deduct 1 point for having only three trumps.

c. 8 points. Primary. *Bid 2 Diamonds*. Same rule as "a" above.

d. 6 points. Primary. *Bid 1 No Trump*. You can't support your partner's suit, you can't bid a suit of your own at a one level, but you have 6 points in high cards and you must bid *1 No Trump*.

Hand #3   ♠ x x   ♡ Q x x x   ◇ A x x   ♣ x x x x

a. Partner opens with *1 Heart*
   Your points_____ Group_____ Your *Response*_____?

b. Partner opens with *1 Diamond*
   Your points_____ Group_____ Your *Response*_____?

c. Partner opens with *1 Club*
   Your points_____ Group_____ Your *Response*_____?

d. Partner opens with *1 Spade*
   Your points_____ Group_____ Your *Response*_____?

ANSWERS

Hand #3

a. 8 points. Primary. *Bid 2 Hearts*. Promote the Queen of Hearts to 3 points.

b. 6 points. Primary. *Bid 2 Diamonds*. The Ace of Diamonds counts 4 points already so you wouldn't promote it, *but* you must deduct 1 point for having only three trumps.

c. 7 points. Primary. *Bid 2 Clubs*.

d. 6 points. Primary. *Bid 1 No Trump*. Since partner bid Spades and you do not have a suit of your own, you do not count the distributional point in Spades. The 6 points are in high cards.

Hand #4   ♠ x x x x   ♡ K J x x x   ◇ Q x x   ♣ x

a. Partner opens with *1 Spade*
   Your points_____ Group_____ Your *Response*_____?

b. Partner opens with *1 Heart*
   Your points_____ Group_____ Your *Response*_____?

c. Partner opens with *1 Club*
   Your points_____ Group_____ Your *Response*_____?

d. Partner opens with *1 Diamond*
   Your points_____ Group_____ Your *Response*_____?

ANSWERS

Hand #4

a. 9 points. Primary. *Bid 2 Spades*. Since you can support your partner's Spades, you must promote the singleton to 3 points.

b. 9 points. Primary. *Bid 2 Hearts*. Promote the singleton to 3 points. You already have 4 points in your Heart suit so you do not promote the honors.

c. 8 points. Primary. *Bid 1 Heart*. You can't raise partner's suit, but you have a suit of your own so you will count your singleton as 2 points. You promise your partner 6 to 18 points and you will tell him more on your *Rebid*. This is a 1 over 1 bid and your partner must bid again.

d. 8 points if you bid a Heart. Primary. *Bid 1 Heart*. Again you promise 6 to 18 points. You have adequate trump support for Diamonds, however, you have only one convenient bid, and I would prefer showing the major suit. Your partner could have good support for your Heart suit and 16 or 17 points. It takes only 26 points to make a game in Hearts, but it takes 29 points in Diamonds.

CHAPTER IV

Rebids by the Opening Bidder of "1 of a Suit"

Now is the time to be concerned about "grouping" your hand. At this time you will give your partner a more exact picture of your point count. (When you turn on your television set, it usually gives you certain signs of being on, but the picture isn't clear. After a few seconds you get up and work with the controls to get a clearer picture of the program.)

This is what happens between the *Opening Bidder* and the *Responder*. The *Opening Bidder* opens the bidding with one of a suit which says, "Partner, it will be a few seconds before I can give you a clear picture of my hand. If you will give me a chance to *Rebid*, I will tell you in which 'group' my hand lies."

POINT TO REMEMBER

If your rebid proves embarrassing, then you should have passed OR you opened with the wrong suit. This will be discussed more thoroughly in the chapter "Which Suit To Bid First."

REBIDDING WITH 13, 14, AND 15 POINT JUNIOR HIGH HANDS

There are only four convenient ways to tell your partner on your *rebid* that you have a *Junior High Hand* with only 13, 14 or 15 points:

1. *Raise your partner's suit.*

2. *Rebid your own suit.*

YOUR REBID CLEARS THE PICTURE.

3. *Rebid 1 No Trump.*

4. *Rebid a lower-ranking suit or sneak in a bid. (Shows 13 to 21 points.)*

5. *Pass. (Only after response of a raise or 1 No Trump.)*

EXAMPLES

1. *Raise your partner's suit.*

    As South you hold:

    ♠ K x x   ♡ x x x   ◇ K Q   ♣ A J x x x (13 points)

    The bidding:

    South *Opens* with *1 Club*.   North *Responds* with *1 Spade*.

    South *Rebids 2 Spades.* (13 points in support of Spades)

Message:

"Partner, I have a Junior High hand with 13, 14 or 15 points. You named a new suit so I have to bid again. Since I have adequate trump support, I will raise your suit. Please don't expect much more from me because I have given you a picture of my hand to within 3 points."

2. *Rebid your own suit.*

    As South you hold:

    ♠ K x x   ♡ x x x   ◇ K Q   ♣ A J x x x (Same hand)

    The bidding:

    South *Opens* with *1 Club*.   North *Responds* with *1 Diamond*,

    South *Rebids 2 Clubs.*

Message:

"Partner, I have a Junior High hand with 13, 14 or 15 points. I realize that I have to bid again because you may have as many as 18 points. I do not have adequate trump support for your suit. I can't *Rebid 1 No Trump* because I don't have guarded honors in Hearts, so I must rebid my *Rebiddable* Club suit."

[39]

3. *Rebid 1 No Trump.* (This is a true No Trump. Your partnership must have guarded honors in all four suits.)

As South you hold:

♠ K x x   ♡ x x x   ◇ K Q   ♣ A J x x x (Same hand)

The bidding:

South *Opens* with *1 Club.*   North *Responds* with *1 Heart.*

South *Rebids 1 No Trump.*

Message:

"Partner, I have a Junior High hand with 13, 14 or 15 points. Since you named a new suit, I have to bid again. I can't raise your suit because I don't have adequate trump support. Now that you have told me you have guarded honors in Hearts I prefer *Rebidding 1 No Trump* because my Club suit isn't very solid. (By being solid I mean A K Q x x.) You, of course, realize that I have guarded honors in the unmentioned Diamond and Spade suits or 1 wouldn't have bid the No Trump."

4. *Rebid a lower-ranking suit or sneak in a bid. (Shows 13 to 21 points.)*

As South you hold:

♠ A Q x x x   ♡ K Q x x   ◇ x x   ♣ x x (13 points)

The bidding:

South *Opens* with *1 Spade.*   North *Responds* with *2 Clubs.*

South *Rebids 2 Hearts.*

Message:

"Partner, I don't promise any more than my original 13 points. If I had *Rebid 2 Spades* I would have shown a minimum hand, right? Can't I sneak in this Heart bid just as cheap as rebidding 2 Spades? If you don't like the Heart suit can't you say *2 Spades* as well as I? If you don't like either one of my suits you could take a preference to my first suit, assuming that it is longer. I could have a very good hand, however, and still have to bid in the same manner. For example:

♠ A K Q x x   ♡ A K J x   ◇ x x   ♣ x x (19 points)

Wouldn't I have to bid this hand the same way? Obviously, *sneaking in a bid doesn't show any additional values but could be a hand just under an opening 2 bid."*

5. *Pass.*

As South you hold:

♠ K x x   ♡ x x x   ♢ K Q   ♣ A J x x x (Same hand)

The bidding:

South *Opens* with *1 Club.*   North *Responds* with *2 Clubs* or

South *Rebids* with a *Pass.*   *1 No Trump.*

Message:

"Partner, since you *Responded* with *1 No Trump* or *raised my suit,* I know that your hand is limited to 9 points. I have added your possible 9 points to my 13 points, and they do not add up to 26 points which is necessary for us to make a game (see Chapter XIV on "Scoring") so I want to pass as soon as possible. If I bid again, you will think I'm pushing and with 8 or 9 points you will bid again, and we will be two tricks too high instead of one. When I pass, it is obvious that I have a Junior High hand with only 13, 14 or 15 points.

HOW TO RE-EVALUATE THE OPENING BIDDER'S HAND AFTER PARTNER HAS RESPONDED

1. If you are able to raise the *Responder's* suit (with adequate trump support), then you must *promote* honors and distributional points just as if *you* were the *Responder.* (See Page 37.)

2. If your partner has raised your suit (any time during the bidding), then you must add the following points:

1 extra point for having a five-card suit.

3 extra points for having a six-card suit.

5 extra points for having a seven-card suit.

7 extra points for having an eight-card suit, etc.

(In other words add 1 point for your fifth trump and 2 for each trump thereafter.) *IMPORTANT:* Your point count changes *only* when you are *together* with your partner; i.e., when you can support his suit or when he has supported your suit.

Note: Let me insert a couple of helpful hints at this point.

(1) As the opening bidder, if you have all of the Aces in your hand, wouldn't you be happy? Well, just express yourself by adding a point to your hand: however, if you haven't any Aces at all, it would make you sad, so just reduce your hand 1 point to show your displeasure.

(2) Another kind of hand that would make you want to express yourself, either as the Opening Bidder or the Responder, would be a hand with no distributional points, so just do so by deducting a point from your hand.

QUIZ

In the following hands you are North. South is your partner. East and West are your opponents who pass in all situations. What is your *Rebid?*

Hand #1   ♠ A J x   ♡ K Q x x x   ◇ x x x   ♣ A x

        Points_____   Group_____

  a. North bids *1 Heart.* South bids *1 Spade.*
    Rebid points_____?   North *Rebids*_____?

  b. North bids *1 Heart.* South bids *2 Diamonds.*
    Rebid points_____?   North *Rebids*_____?

  c. North bids *1 Heart.* South bids *2 Hearts.*
    Rebid points_____?   North *Rebids*_____?

  d. North bids *1 Heart.* South bids *1 No Trump.*
    Rebid points_____?   North *Rebids*_____?

ANSWERS

15 points   Junior High group

a. 14 rebid points. You are together with your partner but since you have only three trumps, you must deduct 1 point. Junior High hand. *Rebid 2 Spades.*

b. 15 rebid points. Junior High hand. *Rebid 2 Hearts.* To rebid *2 No Trump* would indicate guarded honors in each suit but would also indicate 16 points in high cards and you have only 14.

c. 16 rebid points. You are together with your partner so add 1 point for the fifth Heart after your partner raises. You now have a High School hand. *Pass.* Your 16 points and your partner's possible 9 points do not add up to 26 points which are necessary to make a game in Hearts.

d. 14 rebid points in high cards. Junior High hand. *Pass.* Your 14 points and your partner's possible 9 points do not add up to the 26 points necessary for game in No Trump or in Hearts. Your problem is whether to leave the bid at *1 No Trump* or to rebid your Hearts. Where will it play better? I would prefer the No Trump because your *Heart* suit is not very solid. You will have to take only seven tricks at *1 No Trump*, and eight tricks at a *2 Heart* contract.

Hand #2   ♠ x x x   ♡ Q J x   ◇ x x   ♣ A K Q x x

Points_____   Group_____

a. North bids *1 Club*. South bids *1 Spade*.
Rebid points_____?   North *Rebids*_____?

b. North bids *1 Club*. South bids *1 Diamond*.
Rebid points_____?   North *Rebids*_____?

c. North bids *1 Club*. South bids *2 Clubs*.
Rebid points_____?   North *Rebids*_____?

d. North bids *1 Club*. South bids *1 No Trump*.
Rebid points_____?   North *Rebids*_____?

[43]

13 points   Junior High hand

a. 13 rebid points. Junior High hand. *Rebid 2 Clubs.*

b. 13 rebid points. Junior High hand. *Rebid 2 Clubs.*

c. 14 rebid points. You are together with your partner so add 1 for the fifth trump after your partner has raised. Junior High hand. *Pass.* Your 14 points and partner's possible 9 points do not add up to 29, which is necessary to make a game in a minor suit.

d. 13 rebid points (for a Club rebid). Junior High hand. *Rebid 2 Clubs.* You have a worthless doubleton, a good solid suit of your own, so rebid your Clubs rather than leave it at *1 No Trump.*

Hand #3 ♠ K Q J x x ♡ A x x ◇ K x x ♣ x x

   Points_____ Group_____

a. North bids *1 Spade.* South bids *2 Spades.*
 Rebid points_____? North *Rebids*_____?

b. North bids *1 Spade.* South bids *2 Clubs.*
 Rebid points_____? North *Rebids*_____?

c. North bids *1 Spade.* South bids *1 No Trump.*
 Rebid points_____? North *Rebids*_____?

d. North bids *1 Spade.* South bids *2 Hearts.*
 Rebid points_____? North *Rebids*_____?

ANSWERS

14 points   Junior High hand

a. 15 rebid points. Since you are together with your partner, add 1 point for the fifth trump after your partner has raised. Junior High hand. *Pass.* No game in sight.

b. 14 rebid points. Junior High hand. *Rebid 2 Spades.* You do not have adequate trump support for your partner. Now that

[44]

your partner has bid Clubs, you have a guarded honor in each suit, but you would have to rebid *2 No Trump*. (A rebid of *1 No Trump* indicates a Junior High hand, not *2 No Trump*).

c. 14 rebid points (for Spade rebid). Junior High hand. *Rebid 2 Spades* (you have a worthless doubleton).

d. 13 rebid points. You are together with your partner but since you have only three trumps, you must deduct 1 point. Junior High hand, *Rebid 3 Hearts*. When your partner bids at a two level, he tells you that he has 10 points. Don't be afraid to bid 3. You have 24 points between the partnership. If he has additional points, he will go to *4 Hearts* (game in Hearts).

Hand #4   ♠ A J x   ♡ J x x x   ◇ x   ♣ K Q x x x

Points_____   Group_____

a. North bids *1 Club*. South bids *2 Clubs*.
Rebid points_____?   North *Rebids*_____?

b. North bids *1 Club*. South bids *1 Spade*.
Rebid points_____?   North *Rebids*_____?

c. North bids *1 Club*. South bids *1 Heart*.
Rebid points_____?   North *Rebids*_____?

d. North bids *1 Club*. South bids *1 Diamond*.
Rebid points_____?   North *Rebids*_____?

ANSWERS

13 points   Junior High hand

a. 14 rebid points. You are together with your partner so add 1 extra point for the fifth trump after your partner raises your suit. Junior High hand. *Pass*. No game in sight.

b. 13 rebid points. Since you are together with your partner and can support his Spades, your singleton gets 3 points instead of 2. However, you have to deduct a point for having only three trumps. Junior High hand. *Rebid 2 Spades*. Your partner could have as many as 18 points with his *1 over 1* bid, and you can't pass him.

[45]

c. 15 rebid points. Since you are together with your partner and can support his Heart bid, you promote the Jack of Hearts 1 point, giving it 2 instead of 1. Since you have four trumps, you don't have to deduct a point. Promote the singleton to 3 points. Junior High hand. *Rebid 2 Hearts.* Your partner could have 18 points. Don't pass him.

d. 13 rebid points. Junior High hand. Your partner has told you that he has from 6 to 18 points so you must bid again. I would just *Rebid 2 Clubs.* If your partner bids again, you can bid *No Trump* since your partner has bid your singleton.

REBIDDING WITH 16-, 17-, AND 18-POINT HIGH SCHOOL HANDS

YOU HAVE OPENED THE BIDDING WITH 1 OF A SUIT

To show your High School hand with 16, 17 or 18 points, you should *Rebid* in one of the following ways, depending upon the type of hand that you hold:

1. *Jump in your own suit.*

2. *Jump in your partner's suit.*

3. *Rebid 2 No Trump (without jumping).*

4. *Rebid at the three-level.*

5. *Rebid a lower-ranking suit or sneak in a bid. (Shows 13 to 21 points.)*

EXAMPLES

1. *Jump in your own suit.*

As South you hold:

♠ x x   ♡ A K J x x x   ◇ K Q x   ♣ K x

The bidding:

South *Opens* with *1 Heart.*   North *Responds* with *1 Spade.* South *Rebids 3 Hearts.*

     (18 points)

Message:

"Partner, I have a High School hand with 16, 17 or 18 points. I have a *six-card suit* or a *good solid five-card suit.*" (A K Q x x)

2. *Jump in your partner's suit.*

As South you hold:

♠ J x x x   ♡ A Q x x x   ◇ A K   ♣ x x

The bidding:

South *Opens* with *1 Heart.*   North *Responds* with *1 Spade.*

South *Rebids 3 Spades.*
    (17 points)

Message:

"Partner, I have a High School hand with 16, 17 or 18 points, and I have *more than* adequate trump support." (Either an honor and three small cards or four small cards.)

3. *Rebid 2 No Trump (without jumping).*

As South you hold:

♠ A J x x x   ♡ K x   ◇ A J x   ♣ K J x

The bidding:

South *Opens* with *1 Spade.*   North *Responds* with *2 Hearts.*

South *Rebids 2 No Trump.*
    (17 points)

Message:

"Partner, I have a High School hand with 16, 17 or 18 points. Between the two of us we have guarded honors in all four suits."

Note: If you had not had 16 points, you would have *Rebid* your Spade suit to show a minimum hand.

4. *Rebid at the three-level.*

As South you hold:

♠ A Q x x x   ♡ x   ◇ A J x x x   ♣ K x

The bidding:

South *Opens* with *1 Spade*.   North *Responds* with *2 Hearts*.
South *Rebids 3 Diamonds*.
        (17 points)

Message:

"Partner, I have *two biddable suits in my hand*, and I have a High School hand with 16, 17 or 18 points. If I had not had 16 points in my hand, I would have bid the hand differently, so as not to show my second suit at the *three level*, or I would have *Rebid* my Spade suit."

> 5. *Rebid a lower-ranking suit or sneak in a bid. (Shows 13 to 21 points. See #4, page 47.)*

REBIDDING WITH 19-, 20-, AND 21-POINT COLLEGE HANDS

YOU HAVE OPENED THE BIDDING WITH 1 OF A SUIT

To show your College hand with 19, 20 or 21 points, you should *Rebid* in one of the following ways, depending upon the type of hand that you hold:

(Notice the similarity between the *Rebid of the High School hand and the College hand.*)

> 1. *Double jump in your own suit.*
>
> 2. *Double jump in partner's suit.*
>
> 3. *Jump in No Trump.* (In your High School hand you just *Rebid 2 No Trump without jumping*, but notice in the College hand you *Jump* in No Trump. This will be discussed further in Chapter VIII on No Trump Bids.)
>
> 4. *Rebid a higher-ranking suit (which forces your partner to the three level when he wants to show a preference to your first suit).*

EXAMPLES

> 1. *DOUBLE jump in your own suit.*
>
> As South you hold:
>
> ♠ x x   ♡ A K Q J x x   ◇ K Q x   ♣ K x

[48]

The bidding:

South *Opens* with *1 Heart*.   North *Responds* with *1 Spade*.

South *Rebids 4 Hearts*.
    (20 points)

Message:

"Partner, I have a College hand with 19, 20 or 21 points. I have a good solid five-card suit or a six-card suit. Since you have shown me at least 6 points and it takes only 26 points to make a game in Hearts, I must bid the game (4 Hearts) because you might pass the next time."

2. *DOUBLE jump in partner's suit.*

As South you hold:

♠ J x x x   ♡ A K Q J x   ♢ K Q   ♣ K x

The bidding:

South *Opens* with *1 Heart*.   North *Responds* with *1 Spade.*

South *Rebids 4 Spades*.
    (21 points)

Message:

"Partner, I have a College hand with 19, 20 or 21 points. I have *more than* adequate trump support for your suit and since it takes only 26 points to make a game in spades, I must bid the game (4 Spades) because you may have only 6 points and pass the next time."

3. *Jump in No Trump.*

As South you hold:

♠ K x x   ♡ A K J x x   ♢ K Q   ♣ A x x

                or

♠ A Q x   ♡ A Q J x x   ♢ x x x   ♣ A K

The bidding:

South *Opens* with *1 Heart*.   North *Responds* with *2 Diamonds*.

South *Rebids 3 No Trump*.
    (20 points in either hand)

Message:

"Partner, I have a College hand with 19, 20 or 21 points. My hand was too strong to *Open* the bidding with *1 No Trump* and not strong enough for a *2 No Trump* bid (see Chapter VIII, on No Trump). In hand #1, I have all four suits guarded. In hand #2, since you *Responded* in my unguarded suit with the 19 to 21 point hand, I can still *jump in No Trump.*"

4. *Rebid a higher-ranking suit (which forces your partner to the three level when he wants to show a preference to your first suit).*

As South you hold:

♠ A Q x x   ♡ A K J x x   ◇ K x x   ♣ x

The bidding:

South *Opens* with *1 Heart.*   North *Responds* with *2 Clubs.*

South *Rebids 2 Spades.*   North *Rebids 3 Hearts.*

Message:

"Partner, did I sneak in a Spade bid? Can you take a preference to my first suit without going to a three level? No? Then I must have a big hand. If I had had five Hearts and four Spades and a minimum hand, I would have had to resort to the 'Liar's code.' "

"Many of my bridge hands do not fit a rule. No matter what I bid on these hands I cannot tell you the truth. According to the 'Liar's Code,' I would rather lie about the *length* of my suits than the *strength* of my hand. When I have five Hearts and four Spades and a minimum hand I just treat them as if they are the same length and bid the Spade suit first. *Note:* See Chapter VII on "Which Suit to Bid First."

REBIDDING WITH 22-POINT (OR MORE) GROWNUP HANDS (SOMETIMES WITH 21 POINTS)

YOU HAVE OPENED THE BIDDING WITH 1 OF A SUIT

Many of your 22-point (Grownup) hands can be shown by *opening the bidding* with *2 in a suit.* (See Chapter IX on Opening 2 Bids.)

[50]

Some 22-point hands, however, do not qualify for an *opening 2 bid,* so they must be shown on your *rebid.*

You show this by a *Jump Shift on the Rebid.*

EXAMPLE

As South you hold:

♠ A Q x x   ♡ A K x x x   ◇ A K x   ♣ x

The bidding:

South *Opens* with *1 Heart.*   North *Responds* with *2 Clubs.*

South *Rebids 3 Spades.*

Message:

"Partner, I have a Grownup hand *with more* than 21 points." That's all there is to it.

SUMMARY:

This is what you should know at this stage of the book.

OPENING A 1 BID SHOWS 13 TO 21 POINTS

Rebid to show (after a 1 over 1 Response):

13, 14 or 15 Points
1. Raise partner's Suit
2. Rebid own suit
3. Rebid 1 No Trump
4. Rebid a lower-ranking suit or sneak in a bid. (Shows 13 to 21 points.)
5. Pass (if RESPONSE is #1 or #2—showing 6, 7, 8 or 9 points)

16, 17 or 18 Points
1. Jump in partner's suit
2. Jump in own suit
3. Rebid 2 No Trump without jumping
4. Rebid at the three level
5. Rebid a lower-ranking suit or sneak in a bid. (Shows 13 to 21 points.)

19, 20 or 21 Points
1. Double jump in partner's suit
2. Double jump in your own suit
3. Jump in No Trump
4. Rebid a higher-ranking suit

22 Points (pushing partner to the three-level when showing a preference)
1. Jump shift on your rebid

RESPONSES

6, 7, 8 or 9 Points
1. Raise partner's Suit
2. Bid 1 No Trump
3. 1 over 1. (Shows 6 to 18 points.)

QUIZ AND ANSWERS

In the following hands you *Open* with *1 Heart*. Your partner *Responds* with *1 Spade*. The opponents pass. What is your rebid?

Hand #1.   ♠ Q x x x   ♡ A K Q x x   ◇ A   ♣ K Q x

Rebid points_____ Group_____ Your rebid_____?

Your partner is showing you from 6 to 18 points when he responds with a 1 over 1.

24 Rebid points.

Grownup hand.

You are together with your partner so your Queen of Spades is promoted to 3 points and your singleton is promoted to 3 points.

You rebid *3 Clubs*, a *Jump Shift Rebid*. You can bid a three-card suit to show this many points. Your partner can't leave you there when you are showing 22 points.

Hand #2.   ♠ K x   ♡ A Q J x x   ◇ A K x   ♣ Q J 10

Rebid points_____ Group_____ Your rebid_____?

20 Rebid points for No Trump rebid.

College Hand.

You rebid *2 No Trump*, a *Jump Rebid* in No Trump.

Hand #3. ♠ K x   ♡ A K Q x x x   ◇ A K x   ♣ x x

  Rebid points_____ Group_____ Your rebid_____?

21 Rebid points.

College Hand.

You rebid *4 Hearts, Double Jump Rebid* in your own suit. Partner shows 6 points added to your 20 is game. Your suit is strong enough to stand alone without support.

Hand #4. ♠ Q x x x   ♡ A K J x x   ◇ x   ♣ K x x

  Rebid points_____ Group_____ Your rebid_____?

17 Rebid points (you are together with your partner).

High School hand.

You rebid *3 Spades, Jump Rebid* in partner's suit.

Hand #5. ♠ J x x x   ♡ A K Q x x   ◇ A K   ♣ x x

  Rebid points_____ Group_____ Your rebid_____?

20 Rebid points (you are together with your partner).

College Hand.

Your rebid is *4 Spades, Double Jump Rebid* in partner's suit. Partner is showing you 6 points added to your 20 is game.

Hand #6. ♠ A x   ♡ A K Q x x x   ◇ Q x x x   ♣ x

  Rebid points_____ Group_____ Your rebid_____?

18 Rebid points.

High School hand.

Your rebid is *3 Hearts, Jump Rebid* in your suit.

Hand #7.   As South you hold:

  ♠ A K J x x   ♡ None   ◇ A J x x x   ♣ Q x x

  South *Opens* with *1 Spade*. North *Responds* with *2 Hearts*.

  Rebid points_____ Group_____ Your rebid_____?

18 Rebid points.

High School hand.

Your rebid is *3 Diamonds*. Rebidding at the three level shows a High School hand with 16, 17 or 18 points.

[53]

Hand #8. As South you hold:

♠ K Q x x x   ♥ K x x   ♦ A K J   ♣ x x

South *Opens* with *1 Spade*. North *Responds* with *2 Clubs*.

Rebid points_____ Group_____ Your rebid_____?

16 Rebid points in No Trump bidding.

High School hand.

Your rebid is *2 No Trump*. Rebidding *2 No Trump* (without jump-ing) shows High School hand with 16, 17 or 18 points.

Hand #9. As South you hold:

♠ A K J x   ♥ K x x   ♦ A Q x x x   ♣ x

South *Opens* with *1 Diamond*. North *Responds* with *2 Clubs*.

Rebid points_____ Group_____ Your rebid_____?

19 Rebid points.

College hand.

You rebid *2 Spades*. You are *Rebidding* a higher-ranking suit, forcing your partner to the three level if he prefers your first suit. This is called a "Reverse Bid" and to do this you must have 19 points.

Hand #10. As South you hold:

♠ A K J x x x   ♥ x x   ♦ A x x   ♣ x

South *Opens* with *1 Spade*. North *Responds* with *2 Spades*.

Rebid points_____ Group_____ Your rebid_____?

20 Rebid points. You are together with your partner. After your partner raises your suit, you must add 1 extra point if you have 5 trumps, 3 extra points if you have 6 trumps, and 5 extra points if you have 7 trumps. In other words, just add 1 point for the fifth trump and 2 more for each trump thereafter.

College hand.

Your rebid is *4 Spades*. Your partner promised you at least 6 points and you now have 20 so bid the game.

CHAPTER V

Bidding and Rebidding by the Responder

REBIDDING THE 6-, 7-, 8- AND 9-POINT PRIMARY HANDS

THE ONLY TIME YOU REBID AFTER YOU HAVE SHOWN THAT YOU HAVE A PRIMARY HAND WITH 6, 7, 8 OR 9 POINTS IS AS FOLLOWS

1. *When you are pushed.*

2. *To show a suit preference.*

1. *When you are pushed.*

   Example of partner *pushing:*

   a. ♠ x x x
      ♡ Q x x x
      ◇ x x
      ♣ K x x x

   Partner opens with—*1 Heart*
   Your points—7
   Group—Primary
   Your *Response—2 Hearts*
   Partner Rebids—3 Hearts
   Your Rebid—Pass

   b. ♠ x x x
      ♡ K Q x x
      ◇ x x
      ♣ K x x x

   Partner opens with—*1 Heart*
   Your points—9
   Group—Primary
   Your *Response—2 Hearts*
   Partner Rebids—3 Hearts
   Your Rebid—4 Hearts

When you bid 2 Hearts, you promised your partner 6, 7, 8, or 9 points, didn't you? If he knows the rules just as you do, he has added his points to those you promised. He knows that it takes 26 points to make a game

[55]

in Hearts and Spades. If he couldn't count enough points between the partnership to make a game, he would have passed. If he needed only 6 or 7 points added to his to make game, he would have bid 4 Hearts himself. So common sense tells you that he wants to know when he bid 3 Hearts whether you had only 6 or 7 points, or whether you had 8 or 9 points. If you have the bottom of your bid, you must pass. If you have the top of your bid, you must go on to 4 Hearts which is game.

2. *To show a suit preference.*

When you have shown your partner only 6, 7, 8, or 9 points as you do when responding with a raise in his suit, or *1 No Trump*, and you rebid in his first suit, you are giving him the following message: "Partner, I told you I had only 6, 7, 8, or 9 points. I haven't any additional points, but I can't let you play the hand in your second suit. According to my hand, you must play it in your first suit."

Example of showing a suit preference:

a. ♠ x x x
  ♡ Q J x x
  ◇ J x x
  ♣ Q x x

Partner opens with *1 Spade*
Your points—6
Group—Primary
Your *Response—1 No Trump*
Partner *Rebids—2 Hearts*
Your Rebid—Pass

b. ♠ x x x
  ♡ Q J x x
  ◇ J x
  ♣ Q x x x

Partner opens with *1 Spade*
Your points—6
Group—Primary
Your *Response—1 No Trump*
Partner *Rebids—2 Diamonds*
Your Rebid—2 Spades

In hand (a) as the *Responder*, you liked Hearts better than Spades, so you left him in his second suit. His first bid suit is usually better than his second, but since you like Hearts much better, you will want to leave him there.

In hand (b) you like his Spade suit better because you have more cards in that suit. He probably does, too, from the way that he bid. Did you notice that you didn't have to raise the bid level? The *Responder* showed a preference of suits in both hands.

RESPONDING AND REBIDDING WITH THE 10-, 11-, AND 12-POINT INTERMEDIATE HANDS

These hands are beginning to grow up just a little. They *sometimes* have *two bids*. Of course, the 10-point hands can't go as far as the 11- or 12-point hands because they have just gotten out of the Primary department.

There are only two ways to show the Intermediate Hands:

1. Respond at the *two level*. (Showing 10 to 18 points.)

2. Respond with a *1 over 1*. (Showing 6 to 18 points.)

EXAMPLES

1. Responding at the *two level*. (Showing 10 to 18 points.)

   As South you hold:

   ♠ Q x x x   ♡ K Q x x x   ◇ x x x   ♣ x

   The bidding:

   North *Opens* with *1 Spade*.   Your *Response* is *2 Hearts*.

   You have 11 points in support of Spades.

Message:

"Partner, I have at least 10 points in my hand when I bid at a *two level*. I could have as many as 18 so you must *bid again* and give me a chance to 'group' my hand."

Note: To bid this hand, you will raise Spades on the next bid. This sequence of bidding will tell your partner that your hand is in the Intermediate range and that you had more than 10 points. A 10-point hand has only one bid if you bid a *2 over 1* because you have already shown 10 points.

2. Responding with a *1 over 1*. (Showing 6 to 18 points.)

   Let's change the above hand just a little.

   As South you hold:

   ♠ K Q x x x   ♡ Q x x x   ◇ x x x   ♣ x

The bidding:

North *Opens* with *1 Heart.*   Your *Response* is *1 Spade.*

You still have 11 points in support of partner's suit, but this time, you can name your suit at the *one level* instead of two. This shows 6 to 18 points.

Message:

"Partner, I have at least 6 points and a possible 18 points. Please bid again and give me a chance to show you which 'group' my hand is in on my *Rebid.*"

Note: When you make a *1 over 1 bid* with 10, 11 or 12 points, you have *two* convenient bids. You should raise your partner's Hearts on your rebid.

RESPONDING AND REBIDDING WITH THE 13-, 14- AND 15-POINT JUNIOR HIGH HANDS

A Junior High hand facing a Junior High hand will normally produce a game in a major suit or No Trump. (Junior High boys and girls are beginning to step out together. A movie, a bowling date, or a party at a friend's home adds up to a "wonderful time." Any bridge team has a wonderful time when they can bid and make a game.)

There are four ways to show this group.

1. *Jump raise in partner's suit.*

2. *Jump in No Trump.*

3. *1 over 1.*

4. *2 over 1.*

EXAMPLES

1. *Jump raise in partner's suit.* (1 Spade—3 Spades.)

As South you hold:

♠ K x x x   ♡ x x   ◇ A K x   ♣ Q J x x

The bidding:

North *Opens* with *1 Spade.* Your *Response* is *3 Spades.*

(15 points)

Message:

"Partner, I have a Junior High hand with 13, 14 or 15 points (sometimes 16) and I have *more than adequate trump support*, i.e., an *honor* with three small cards or *five small cards*. Since you had to have 13 points to *open* the bidding and I have 13, we have a game. You must bid again so we will not stop short of the game. Since we have established our suit, if either one of us bids a side suit, we are showing Aces in that suit."

2. *Jump in No Trump.* (1 Spade—2 No Trump.)

As South you hold:

♠ x x   ♡ K x x   ◇ A Q x x   ♣ K J x x

The bidding:

North *Opens* with *1 Spade.*   Your *Response* is *2 No Trump.*
   (13 points)

Message:

"Partner, I have a Junior High hand with 13, 14 or 15 points. I also have guarded honors in the three unbid suits. If I had just 1 more point (16) than the Junior High maximum, I would have bid *3 No Trump* instead of 2, so you see this bid is very descriptive. Since you had to have 13 points to open the bid, you must bid again or we will miss a game and lose a lot of points."

3. *1 over 1, or 2 over 1.* (6 to 18 points, or 10 to 18 points.)

As South you hold:

(a)   ♠ A K Q x x   ♡ Q x x   ◇ x x x x   ♣ x
                          or
(b)   ♠ Q x x   ♡ A K Q x x   ◇ x x x x   ♣ x

The bidding:

In hand (a) your partner *Opened* with *1 Heart* so your *Response* would be a *1 over 1* (1 Spade with 13 points) and you would bid a game in Hearts on your next bid, if your partner *Rebids* his Heart suit. If he raises your Spades, then rebid a game in Spades.

In hand (b) your partner *Opened* with *1 Spade*, so your *Response* would *have* to be a *2 over 1* (2 Hearts). You have 13 points and you would bid a game in Spades (4 Spades) on your *Rebid*, unless he raised your Heart bid, then bid a game in your Heart suit.

RESPONDING AND REBIDDING WITH THE 16-, 17- AND 18-POINT HIGH SCHOOL HANDS

There is only one descriptive bid in this group. That is the *Jump* to *3 No Trump* instead of *2 No Trump*. The only rule is that all of the three unbid suits are protected by a guarded honor. (See above example for the *Jump in No Trump*.)

The other bids with this High School Hand are the usual *1 over 1*, or the *2 over 1*, which you will have to show on your *Rebid*. As soon as you find a suit fit or No Trump, go to game. *Every time the Responder bids a new suit the opening bidder must bid again.*

RESPONDING AND REBIDDING WITH THE 19-POINT RESPONDER'S GROWNUP HANDS

There is only one bid that describes this hand and that is a *Jump Shift*, e.g., *1 Spade—3 Hearts*. This is the strongest bid the *Responder* can make. You are in *"Slam"** territory.

As South you hold:

♠ K Q J x   ♡ A Q J   ◇ x x x   ♣ A K x

The bidding:

North *Opens* with *1 Spade*. You have 19 points. (Deduct 1 point for having no distributional points.) *Respond* with *3 Hearts*.

Note: This is one of the few times that you will bid a three-card suit, when you are showing points or trying to get to a slam. Partner's

---

* If your partner opens the bidding and you, as *Responder*, are able to give a *Jump Shift* showing 19 points, if you are able to agree on a suit or No Trump, you usually have a slam. It normally takes 33 points to make a *Little Slam* and 37 points to make a *Grand Slam*.

Rebid will determine your next move. Also, it will require reading a few more pages in the book.

JUMPING TO 4 IN A MAJOR SUIT
(BLOCK BIDDING)

As South you hold:

♠ J x x x   ♡ x   ◇ Q x x   ♣ J x x x

The bidding:

North *Opens* with *1 Spade*. East *passes*. Your *Response is 4 Spades*.

Message:

"Partner, I have a weak hand with less than 9 points in high cards. However, I do promise you *five* of your suit and *either a singleton or a void*. Oh, yes, I know that we may not make our bid *but* if we go set our opponents probably had a game bid. If you had a weak opening bid and East didn't have enough points to come into the bidding, with my few points West is just waiting to bid, right? Now, I have made it very difficult for him to communicate with his partner. If this isn't the case then we should make our *4 Spade* bid."

LITTLE SLAM

When six of a suit or No Trump has been bid, it is called a *Little Slam*. *Twelve* tricks have to be taken by *Declarer* in order to make the bid. A *Little Slam* bid and made gives you considerable bonus points. (See scoring chart.) Besides needing 33 points between the partnership, you will also need *three Aces*.

GRAND SLAM

When seven of a suit or No Trump has been bid, it is called a *Grand Slam*. All thirteen tricks have to be taken by *Declarer*. Besides having 37 points, you also need *all four Aces* and three Kings.

Now is the time for you to learn how to find out the number of Aces and Kings your partner has. It is a conventional bid called *Blackwood*.

BLACKWOOD CONVENTION

If you want to know how many Aces partner has, just bid 4 No Trump. This is the *Blackwood Convention* and it asks partner a question: "How many Aces do you have?" If partner has none or all of the Aces he will say 5 Clubs. If he has one Ace he will say 5 Diamonds. If he has two Aces he will say 5 Hearts, and three Aces, 5 Spades.

No doubt you are wondering when a 5 Club response by Partner means *no Aces* or all *four Aces*. If you have at least one Ace, then he couldn't mean all of them, could he? If you have none at all, then your points must be in Kings, Queens, and Jacks; right? If Partner has no Aces at all, then minus your Kings, Queens and Jacks, how do you think he made his bid if he didn't have at least one Ace?

After you have found all four Aces between the partnership, and you want to find out how many Kings partner has, you will bid 5 No Trump. If Partner has none or all, he will say 6 Clubs. One King, he will say 6 Diamonds, two Kings, 6 Hearts, and three Kings, 6 Spades.

If you happen to have all four Aces and *all you want to know* is how many Kings Partner has, you must *first go through the 4 No Trump bid*, asking for Aces, before bidding 5 No Trump, asking for Kings.

Let's assume you bid 4 No Trump, asking Partner how many Aces he has. After the Response, you find that you do not have enough Aces between the partnership to bid 6 (the Little Slam); what do you do? You just return to 5 of your own suit.

Suppose, however, the hand will play better at 5 No Trump than at 5 of a suit. How can you "sign off" at 5 No Trump? If you bid 5 No Trump, Partner will start telling you how many Kings he has, which will result in an unmakable contract. There is a very simple solution. Just name the unbid suit and Partner will take the bid to 5 No Trump. Not your partner, you say? He will if he is thinking. Why would you name a new suit at such a high level of bidding if you weren't trying to get yourself out of a bad situation? If Partner isn't thinking today, he probably won't understand your other bids either.

SUMMARY:

This is what you should know at this stage of the book.

OPENING A 1 BID SHOWS 13 TO 21 POINTS

Rebid to show (after a 1 over 1 response):

13, 14 or 15 Points
1. Raise partner's suit
2. Rebid own suit
3. Rebid 1 No Trump
4. Rebid a lower-ranking suit or sneak in a bid. (Shows 13 to 21 points.)
5. Pass (if RESPONSE is #1 or #2—showing 6, 7, 8 or 9 points)

16, 17 or 18 Points
1. Jump in partner's suit
2. Jump in own suit
3. Rebid 2 No Trump without jumping
4. Rebid at the three level
5. Rebid a lower-ranking suit

19, 20 or 21 Points
1. Double jump in partner's suit
2. Double jump in your own suit
3. Jump in No Trump
4. Rebid a higher-ranking suit (pushing partner to the three level, showing a preference)

22 Points
1. Jump shift on your rebid

RESPONSES

6, 7, 8 or 9 Points
1. Raise partner's suit
2. Bid 1 No Trump
3. 1 over 1. (Shows 6 to 18 points.)

10, 11 or 12 Points
1. 1 over 1. (Shows 6 to 18 points.)
2. 2 over 1. (Shows 10 to 18 points.)

13, 14 or 15 Points
1. 1 over 1. (Shows 6 to 18 points.)
2. 2 over 1. (Shows 10 to 18 points.)
3. Jump in partner's suit
4. Jump in No Trump

16, 17 or 18 Points
1. 1 over 1. (Shows 6 to 18 points.)
2. 2 over 1. (Shows 10 to 18 points.)
3. Jump to 3 No Trump

19 Points
1. Jump shift

QUIZ

Hand #1   ♠ Q x   ♡ K Q x x x   ◇ J x x   ♣ x x x

a. Partner opens with *1 Club*
Your points_____ Group_____ Your *Response*_____?

ANSWERS

a. 8 points. (Deduct 1 point from the Queen of Spades because the honor is unguarded. Add a point for the doubleton.) Primary hand. *Bid 1 Heart—1 over 1*, promising Partner 6 to 18 points. You will group your hand on your rebid, which will probably be a pass.

Hand #2   ♠ K x x x   ♡ Q J x x   ◇ A K x   ♣ x x

a. Partner opens with *1 Heart*
Your points_____ Group_____ Your *Response*_____?

b. Partner opens with *1 Spade*
Your points_____ Group_____ Your *Response*_____?

c. Partner opens with *1 Club*
Your points_____ Group_____ Your *Response*_____?

ANSWERS

a. 15 points. (Add 1 point for the honor in Hearts.) Junior High hand. *Bid 3 Hearts*. Describing an opening bid and more than normal trump support.

[64]

b. 15 points. (Add 1 point for your honor in Spades.) Junior High hand. *Bid 3 Spades.* Describing an opening bid and more than normal trump support.

c. 13 points. You can't count the distribution point in No Trump bidding. Junior High hand. Bid *2 No Trump.* Describing an opening bid and the three unbid suits stopped with guarded honors.

Hand #3 ♠ x x ♡ Q J x x ◇ K J x ♣ A Q x x

a. Partner opens with *1 Spade*
   Your points_____ Group_____ Your *Response*_____?

b. Partner opens with *1 Heart*
   Your points_____ Group_____ Your *Response*_____?

c. Partner opens with *1 Diamond*
   Your points_____ Group_____ Your *Response*_____?

ANSWERS

a. 13 points. No point for the doubleton in No Trump bidding. Junior High hand. *Bid 2 No Trump.* Describing an opening bid with the three unbid suits guarded.

b. 15 points. Add a point to the Heart honor. Junior High hand. *Bid 3 Hearts.* Describing an opening bid with more than adequate trump support.

c. 14 points. Junior High hand. Bid 1 Heart showing 6 to 18 points. If Partner responds with 2 Diamonds, you will rebid 3 Clubs hoping Partner can bid 3 No Trump if he has the Spade suit stopped.

Hand #4 ♠ A K x ♡ x x ◇ K Q J ♣ K J x x x

a. Partner opens with *1 Heart*
   Your points_____ Group_____ Your *Response*_____?

b. Partner opens with *1 Spade*
   Your points_____ Group_____ Your *Response*_____?

c. Partner opens with *1 Diamond*
   Your points_____ Group_____ Your *Response*_____?

[65]

ANSWERS

a. 17 points in No Trump bidding. *Bid 3 No Trump.* Describing a High School hand with 16, 17 or 18 points, and all unbid suits stopped (well guarded).

b. 17 points in support of Spades. (You must deduct 1 point for having only three trumps.) High School hand. *Bid 2 Clubs,* showing 10 to 18 points. You can count 30 points if Partner has his minimum number of points to open his bid. If he rebids anything other than a Junior High hand, you will have a *Slam.* His next bid will determine your rebid. It will *probably* be game in Spades or *Slam.*

c. 17 points in support of Diamonds. High School hand. *Bid 2 Clubs.* You will raise Diamonds later. If Partner bids the Hearts, then you should bid No Trump. (Slam possibilities.)

Hand #5   ♠ A K J x   ♡ x x   ◇ K Q J   ♣ A J x x

a. Partner opens with *1 Spade*
    Your points_____ Group_____ Your *Response*_____?

b. Partner opens with *1 Heart*
    Your points_____ Group_____ Your *Response*_____?

ANSWERS

a. 20 points. Responder's Grownup hand. *Bid 3 Clubs*—a *Jump Shift* showing 19 points or more. The strongest bid Responder can make. If partner rebids a minimum hand, you will still want to go to a *Little Slam.* Bid 6 Spades, because with his minimum of 13 points and your 20 points, it adds up to 33, which should normally produce a *Little Slam.* To make a *Little Slam,* Partner must have at least one Ace, so you will want to bid the "Blackwood Convention" to find out. This convention is designed to keep you out of a *Slam* when you don't belong there.

b. 20 points. Responder's Grownup hand. *Bid 2 Spades. Jump Shift.* You probably have a *Slam.* Await developments by Partner to determine your next bid. (See above answer.)

Hand #6   ♠ K Q J   ♡ K Q J x   ◇ A J   ♣ Q J x x

   a. Partner opens with *1 Club*
      Your points_____ Group_____ Your *Response*_____?

ANSWERS

   a. 21 points in support of Clubs. Add 1 point to the Club honors.
   Responder's Grownup hand. *Bid 2 Hearts, a Jump Shift* bid.
   If Partner rebids Clubs, go to the Blackwood Convention. If
   you have three Aces between the partnership, go to *6 Clubs.*
   If he doesn't rebid Clubs, you will probably have a *Little Slam*
   somewhere *if* you have the three Aces.

Hand #7   ♠ A K x x x   ♡ x x x   ◇ K Q J   ♣ K x

   a. Partner opens with *1 Club*
      Your points_____ Group_____ Your *Response*_____?

ANSWERS

   a. 17 points. High School hand. *Bid 1 Spade. 1 over 1*, showing
   6 to 18 points. If Partner rebids Clubs, what can you do now?
   Bid the three-card Diamond suit hoping you can get to a No
   Trump. Each time you bid a new suit, you are letting Partner
   know you have more points. He will not leave you there. If you
   don't get to No Trump, then bid game in Clubs. After he has
   rebid his Clubs, you can raise with one less Club.

Hand #8   ♠ A x x   ♡ x x   ◇ K Q J x x   ♣ Q x x

   a. Partner opens with *1 Spade*
      Your points_____ Group_____ Your *Response*_____?

   b. Partner opens with *1 Club*
      Your points_____ Group_____ Your *Response*_____?

ANSWERS

   a. 13 points. Junior High hand. *Bid 2 Diamonds* showing 10 to
   18 points. In support of Spades, you have only 13 points

because you must deduct 1 point for having only three trumps. If partner rebids his Spades showing a five-card suit, your hand will be worth 14 points. With your points added to his, you should have a game somewhere.

b. 13 points. Junior High hand. *Bid 1 Diamond*—a *1 over 1* bid showing 6 to 18 points. Await developments. Remember, it takes 29 points to make a game in the minor suits.

CHAPTER VI

Third- and Fourth-Hand Opening Bids and Responses

Now that you are familiar with *Opening Bids, Responses* and *Rebids by the Opening Bidder*, I must confuse you again by giving you some exceptions. The exceptions will be obvious if you understand the previous chapters. If you don't, just skip this chapter for the time being.

You are *South* and the bidding has gone *Pass, Pass*. Obviously, your partner does not have 13 points, 2 Quick Tricks, and a rebid or he would have bid instead of passing, right? *Now*, some of the rules from pages 18 to 54 do not apply, simply because they wouldn't make much sense. For example:

North *Passes.*   South *Opens 1 Heart.*

North *Responds 2 Spades.*

How many points does the *Responder* have when he makes a *Jump Shift* of 2 Spades over 1 Heart? On page 53 I told you that a *Jump Shift* indicates 19 points. *If North has 19 points why did he pass?* With this many points he would have had his 2 Quick Tricks and a rebid. Obviously, he is trying to say that *he had close to an opening bid and if South has any additional values and a suit fit there is still a play for game.* The same principle applies to the following bids:

North *Passes.*   South *Opens 1 Heart.*

North *Responds 3 Hearts*
 or *2 No Trump.*

North has almost an opening bid and in each bid is indicating the type of hand that he has.

Let's look at *South's* position again.

North *Passes.*   South *Opens 1 Heart.*

North *Responds 1 Spade*
    or *2 Clubs.*

In previous chapters I have explained that *either of these bids made by the Responder* (1 over 1 or 2 over 1) *is forcing*, simply because he could have as many as 18 points. Consequently, *South* would have to supply a *Rebid.* However, since *South* knows that his partner *couldn't* have more than 13 points and pass, there is no game in sight, and if the Spade or Club bid suits him he can *now* pass.

Let's take a look at the *North* position. Suppose he hasn't read this chapter and makes an *"artificial bid"** intending to raise *South's* Heart bid later but *South* passes. The fur will surely fly and all of the bridge teachers and writers will be quoted and misquoted. To keep this from happening, let's just make a policy that *after having previously passed, be sure that you won't be embarrassed if Partner leaves you in your suit.*

Let's consider another bid from the *South* position. *North* and *East* have both passed. As *South,* you have only 11 or 12 points. If neither *North* nor *East* has enough points to open the bidding and your hand is this weak, isn't it possible that *West* will be able to bid? If you have a suit you may now bid it because you do not promise a *REBID.* Many hands do not produce a game, and in bidding with 11 or 12 points in third position you and your partner may be able to put up a good fight for a *"part score."*

Most players, including myself, will not open with less than 13 points in fourth position. Since your partner has announced less than 13

---

* An artificial bid is a bid that sometimes must be made to describe your hand. For example: As Responder you have adequate trump support but too many points to raise your partner. You have no suit to bid and can't bid 2 No Trump. You will bid a three-card suit expecting to raise Partner at your next bid.

points, by passing, you couldn't expect more than a *"part score"* and, who knows, your opponents may have more points than your side and outbid you for the *"part score."*

For the above reasons you still do not promise a *Rebid* in fourth position.

CHAPTER VII

Which Suit to Bid First

BIDDABLE SUITS

Any suit consisting of five or more cards is *Biddable*. Any four-card suit headed by *two* honors is *Biddable*. For example:

A J x x, Q J x x, K J x x, A Q x x, K Q x x, or better.

REBIDDABLE SUITS

Any five-card suit headed by two of the top four honors such as Q J x x x or better is *Rebiddable*.

Any six-card suit headed by a Jack or better is *Rebiddable*. (J x x x x x or better.)

No four-card suit is Rebiddable unless your partner has raised it.

Up to this point you have only been exposed to a hand containing one *Rebiddable* five-card suit. You had so many other new things to confuse you that I wanted to save this one until later. All hands, as you have no doubt observed, are not dealt in such a simple manner. When a hand has more than one *Biddable* suit, it is very important to know the correct sequence of bidding.

There are several rules you can memorize to help you decide which suit to bid first, but then you have to memorize the rules that apply to the exceptions. Why not learn the reason for the rule in the first place, and when that reason doesn't apply, it's bound to be an exception. Right? In order to apply this technique you must be aware of your *Rebid* immediately and what that *Rebid* will do to your partner on his second bid. My main objective in writing this book is to teach you *Rebids immediately*. After you have opened the bid, sometimes it's only a few seconds before you are asked to make a *Rebid*. I don't believe you can learn *all Opening Bids* in one course and *all Rebids* in another course without becoming more confused. It is my opinion that they go together and must be taught together. With this in mind let us examine the following hand:

♠ x   ♡ A Q J x   ◇ K J x x x   ♣ A K x
(20 points)

In observing this hand, you will find a longer suit (Diamonds) and a stronger suit (Hearts). If you recall, when you are the *Declarer* you always want to draw your trumps as soon as possible. The more trumps you have, the fewer your opponents have. Your common sense will tell you then that the length of your suit is more important than the strength, which is *Rule #1.*

Rule #1   Bid Your Longest Suit First.

In the above hand you would bid *1 Diamond* first. Let's go a step further and see what this bid will do to your partner on his *Response,* to you on your *Rebid,* and to your partner on his *Rebid.* This is the secret to this technique.

First, you must assume that your partner will *Respond* in your shortest suit. You must be prepared for the worst response he can make. Can't you also assume that if you have fewer cards in that suit, the chances are that would be his longest suit? With this in mind let's bid *1 Diamond.* The hand belongs to South:

South *Opens* with *1 Diamond.*   North *Responds* with *1 Spade.*

South *Rebids 2 Hearts.*   North *Rebids 3 Diamonds.*

You have forced your partner to the three level when he shows a preference for your first bid suit. Is your hand *strong enough* to do this? Yes. You must have 19 points.

Important: When you force partner to the three level when he shows a preference for your first suit, you must have a College hand. (19 points)

Let's change the strength of the hand and try bidding it by the *Rule*.

♠ x   ♡ A Q x x   ◇ K J x x x   ♣ Q x x
(14 points)

If you bid your *longest* suit first you are going to force your partner to the three level to show a preference as before. Is your hand strong enough? No. We now have to resort to the "Liar's Code."

"Liar's Code": If you have a hand that doesn't fit any bridge rule and any bid or rebid that you make is a lie, you must never lie about the *strength* of your hand, but instead lie about the *length* of your suits.

Let's see how this would work:

South *Opens* with *1 Heart*.   North *Responds* with *1 Spade*.

South *Rebids 2 Diamonds*.   North *Rebids 2 Hearts* (showing a preference for your first suit at the two level instead of three).

You promised Partner four Hearts and four Diamonds (you never promise five of any suit until you rebid it). If you open the Diamond suit first you will have to rebid it to show a minimum hand. You cannot show the Heart suit.

Let's take a few hands and see how many hands will apply to the *Rule*.

♠ A Q 10 x   ♡ A K J x x   ◇ K x   ♣ x x

South *Opens* with *1 Heart*.   North *Responds* with *2 Clubs*.

South *Rebids 2 Spades*.   North *Rebids 3 Hearts* (showing a preference).

This is a very good hand worth 19 points and should be bid the orthodox way. You have pushed your partner to three on his rebid, but this you can afford.

♠ A K x x   ♡ Q x x   ◇ K J x x x   ♣ x

South *Opens* with *1 Diamond*.   North *Responds* with *2 Clubs*.

South *Rebids 2 Spades*.   North *Rebids 3 Diamonds* (showing a preference).

You have pushed your partner too high because your hand is in the minimum range. Let's bid it the other way using the "Liar's Code."

South *Opens* with *1 Spade.*   North *Responds* with *2 Clubs.*

South *Rebids 2 Diamonds.*   North *Rebids 2 Spades* (preference).

Note: A *2 Diamond* bid is just as cheap a rebid as *2 Spades.* This shows a hand of no more than 13 to 15 points; however, it could be a big hand.

♠ A K x x   ♡ x   ◇ K J x x x   ♣ K J x

South *Opens* with *1 Diamond.*   North *Responds* with *1 Heart.*

South *Rebids 1 Spade.*   North can take a preference at a two level.

Had you noticed that in this case the orthodox rule applies with a minimum hand? Let's bid it the other way and see what happens.

South *Opens* with *1 Spade.*   North *Responds* with *2 Hearts.*

South has to *Rebid 3 Diamonds.*

This is obviously the wrong bid.

Important: All College hands with 19, 20 or 21 points should be bid normally. That is, *the longest suit first.* Sometimes, the Junior High hands with 13, 14 or 15 points and the High School hands with 16, 17 or 18 points have to be bid abnormally *if* they force partner to the three-level on his *Rebid,* showing a preference. If the opening bidder is forced to *Rebid* at the three level, he must have at least a High School hand with 16, 17 or 18 points.

Rule #2   *Always Bid a Six-Card Suit Before a Four-Card Suit.*

You can always rebid a six-card suit if you can't conveniently show the four-card suit.

Rule #3   *With a Six-Card Suit and a Five-Card Suit, Bid the Six-Card Suit First, and Then Bid the Five-Card Suit Twice.*

The rule says you bid your longest suit first. Another rule says you can't *Rebid* a four-card suit. Right? Well, if you have bid Diamonds and then bid Hearts *twice,* you had to have a five-card Heart suit, didn't you, or you couldn't have bid it twice. Since your first suit is supposed to be your longest, you must have had more than five cards in your Diamond suit. If your suits had been of equal length, you would have bid the higher-ranking suit first. Do you follow?

Rule #4 If You Have Two Biddable Five-Card Suits, or Two Biddable Six-Card Suits, Bid the Higher-Ranking Suit First (not necessarily the strongest).

Examples and reasons for bidding in this manner:

    ♠ A Q x x x   ♡ x   ◇ A Q x x x   ♣ x x

If you show your higher-ranking suit first, which is Spades, and you get a *2 Heart Response* from your partner, you would then be forced to show your Diamond suit at the three level. Since your hand is not strong enough for a *Rebid* at the three level, you can always *Rebid* your five-card Spade suit. You don't mind suppressing a five-card minor suit but never a five-card major.

    ♠ A Q x x x   ♡ A Q x x x   ◇ Q x   ♣ x

If you bid your Spade suit first, and partner *Responds* in either Clubs or Diamonds, you can bid your Heart suit conveniently.

Rule #5 When You Have More Than One Biddable Four-Card Suit, Bid the Suit BELOW the SHORTEST Suit.

Let's take a few examples:

    ♠ A K 10 x   ♡ x x x   ◇ A Q x x   ♣ J x

Let's bid the four-card Spade suit first and see what happens, assuming partner will bid your shortest suit. This hand belongs to South.

South *Opens* with *1 Spade*.	North *Responds* with *2 Clubs*.
South *Rebids 2 Diamonds*.	North *Rebids 2 Spades* if he takes a preference (not raising the contract).

Let's take the same hand and open with the Diamond suit.

South *Opens* with *1 Diamond*.	North *Responds* with *2 Clubs*.
South *Rebids 2 Spades*.	North has to go to the three level to show a preference for your first suit. This is obviously wrong.

[76]

Suppose, however, Partner was rude enough to *Respond* in *2 Hearts* instead of *2 Clubs*; you would have to show your Diamond suit at the three level, wouldn't you? This would be tragic with a minimum hand and your four-card suit if Partner couldn't support either. In this case, you would have to *Rebid* your four-card Spade suit. I know you would not be telling the truth, but would you if you *Rebid* at the three level? No. I would rather fib a little about the length of my suit than about the strength of my hand.

Note: Sometimes you have to tell a little "white lie" to stay out of trouble. (This "rule" has no age limit.)

Rule #6   "Convenient Club Bid."

These are hands that again require the use of the "Liar's Code." When you make a suit bid you promise your partner four cards in that suit. However, in the following hand, if you open with a Spade you will not have a convenient rebid which will describe the strength of your hand.

♠ A Q x x   ♡ Q x x   ◇ x x x   ♣ A Q x

If you *Bid* a Club, do you have a convenient *Rebid?* Yes.

If Partner *Responds* with *1 Diamond*, your *Rebid* will be *1 Spade*.

If Partner *Responds* with *1 Heart*, your *Rebid* is *1 Spade*.

If Partner *Responds* with *1 Spade*, your *Rebid* is *2 Spades*.

If Partner *Responds* with *1 No Trump* or *2 Clubs*, you must pass.

When you make a "Convenient Club Bid" you should have Q x x or better in that suit, because partner may bid No Trump, expecting you to have control of the Club suit.

When you have opened with a Club, your partner must have four Clubs to raise the suit. Otherwise he treats the bid as if it were a normal opening bid.

QUIZ

In the following hands what is the correct sequence of bidding?

1.   ♠ A K x x   ♡ Q J 10 x x   ◇ Q x   ♣ Q x

2.   ♠ A Q 10 x   ♡ x x   ◇ A Q J x x   ♣ x x

3. ♠ A K x x   ♡ A Q x x   ◇ x x   ♣ J x x

4. ♠ A K x   ♡ K Q x   ◇ Q x x x   ♣ A K x

5. ♠ A 10 x x   ♡ K J x x   ◇ x   ♣ A J x x

6. ♠ x x   ♡ x x   ◇ A K Q x   ♣ A 10 x x x

7. ♠ A Q x x   ♡ K Q x   ◇ x x x   ♣ K x x

8. ♠ Q x   ♡ K x x   ◇ K J x x   ♣ A J x x

9. ♠ A J x x   ♡ x   ◇ K J x x   ♣ Q J x x

10. ♠ x x   ♡ A Q J x   ◇ K 10 x x x   ♣ K x

11. ♠ A K x x   ♡ Q x x x   ◇ K x   ♣ Q x x

12. ♠ x x   ♡ A K x x   ◇ J x x   ♣ A Q x x

13. ♠ K Q x   ♡ x x x   ◇ A Q x   ♣ K x x x

ANSWERS

1. *Bid the Spade suit first.* Treat both suits as if they were of equal length. If you bid the Heart suit first, you may not be able to mention the Spade suit.

2. *Bid the Diamonds first* and just hope your partner will *Respond* with Hearts. (The chances are just as good.) Then you can name your Spade suit without taking up any bidding space.

3. *Bid Spades first,* the suit below the shortest suit. (When the shortest suit is Clubs or Diamonds and there isn't a *Biddable* suit lower, you must go up to the top and come down for your next suit.) This hand is very close to the "Convenient Club Bid."

4. *Bid the "Convenient Club."* If your partner *Responds* in any suit, just *Rebid 2 No Trump.* A jump in No Trump shows 19, 20 or 21 points.

5. *Bid 1 Club,* suit below the shortest suit.

6. *Bid the Diamonds first.* Treat the two suits as four-card suits.

7. *Bid the "Convenient Club."* If your partner *Responds* with *1 Diamond* or *1 Heart* then *Respond* with *1 Spade.* Raise either of the other suits. Pass *1 No Trump* or *2 Clubs.*

8. *Bid 1 Diamond*, the suit below the shortest suit.

9. *Bid 1 Diamond*, the suit below the shortest suit.

10. *Bid 1 Heart.* You can't afford to suppress a good four-card major suit. Besides, the Diamond suit isn't a good *Rebiddable* suit.

11. *Bid the "Convenient Club."* If your partner *Responds* with *1 Diamond,* you will *Rebid 1 Spade.* Raise either of the other two suits and pass a *No Trump* or *2 Club Response.*

12. *Bid 1 Club.* Usually when you have a four-card *Biddable* Heart suit and a four-card *Biddable* Club suit, you will want to bid the Club suit first unless you are pretty sure your partner will *Respond* with a Spade. If your partner *Responds* with *1 Spade* in this hand, just *Rebid 1 No Trump,* because you have a minimum hand.

13. *Bid the "Convenient Club."* Rebid 1 No Trump if your partner *Responds* with *1 Heart.* Raise either of the other suits and pass *1 No Trump* or a *2 Club* bid.

Opening, Responding, and Rebidding No Trump Hands

OPENING WITH 16, 17 AND 18 POINTS.
1 NO TRUMP HANDS

There are three requirements for the *1 No Trump Opening Bid.*

1. At least *three* of the four suits must be protected by guarded honors, i.e.: K x, Q x x, J x x x.
2. All points must be *High-Card Points.*
3. You must have a balanced hand, i.e.:
   a. No voids.
   b. No singletons.
   c. No more than one doubleton and it must be headed by the Queen or better.

RESPONDING TO 1 NO TRUMP WITH A BALANCED HAND

There are *two* requirements for *Responding* with the balanced hand.

1. Count *only* high cards.
2. As the *Responder, just add your points to those promised by the opening No Trump bidder.*

IF THE OPENING BIDDER HAD ONLY 16 POINTS AND—

Your combined number of points equals 26, then, as the *Responder,* bid a game (3 No Trump). You should have 10 points to do this.

Your combined number of points equals 33, then as the *Responder,* bid a *Slam* (6 No Trump). You should have 17 points to do this.

Your combined number of points equals 37, then as the Responder bid a *Grand Slam* (7 No Trump). You should have 21 points to do this.

If, however, the Opening Bidder needs 17 or 18 points to make these above situations possible, then as the Responder you should "Push" as follows:

Bid 2 No Trump, "*Pushing*" him to bid 3 if he *opened* with 17 or 18 points. (The *opening* No Trump bidder should know that if you could not see a possible game, you would have passed his *1 No Trump* and that you are asking for the top of his bid.) As the *Responder*, you will need 8 points to do this.

Bid 4 No Trump, "*Pushing*" him to bid 6 if he *opened* with 17 or 18 points. (The *opening* No Trump bidder should know that if you could count only 26 points, you would have bid only 3. His common sense will tell him that you are "*Pushing*" for a *Little Slam* if he has 17 or 18 points.) As the *Responder,* you will need 16 points to do this.

Bid 5 No Trump, "*Pushing*" him to bid 7 if he *opened* with 17 or 18 points. (If the *opening* No Trump bidder knows the above rule, he will be curious as to why you bid *5 No Trump* instead of 4. His common sense will tell him that you must be "*Pushing*" for *7 No Trump.*) As the *Responder* you should have 20 points to do this. (If you do not have the points to bid *7 No Trump* you should bid *6 No Trump.*)

REBIDDING BY THE 1 NO TRUMP OPENER AFTER PARTNER HAS RESPONDED WITH A BALANCED HAND

With 16 points:

Pass. You're already relayed this message to your partner when you opened the bidding with *1 No Trump.* If you bid again, you are telling him that you have additional points.

[81]

With 17 or 18 points:

When Partner responds with *2 No Trump,* then bid *3 No Trump.*

When Partner responds with *4 No Trump,* then bid *6 No Trump.*

When Partner responds with *5 No Trump,* then bid *7 No Trump.*
(With only 16 points, bid *6 No Trump.*)

WITH FIVE-CARD MAJOR SUIT AND 10 POINTS
BID 3 OF SUIT

Now, suppose you have a five-card major suit (or longer) and have enough points to make a game (which is 10 points). Instead of bidding 3 No Trump you will bid 3 of your major suit. Now, the opening bidder will either rebid 3 No Trump, if yours is his weak suit, or raise your major suit to a game. He will not pass.

IF IT'S A MINOR SUIT, BID 3 NO TRUMP

If your five-card suit is a minor suit, you should bid 3 No Trump immediately. This is a gambling bid but it takes 5 of a minor suit to make a game and if you can't make 3 No Trump, you probably couldn't have made 5 of a minor suit either.

WITH 8 OR 9 POINTS AND MAJOR SUIT USE
2 CLUB BID FIRST

If you have 8 or 9 points and a five-card major suit, you will bid the 2 Club Convention first, which asks partner if he has a four-card major suit, and no matter what his response is, you will return to your major suit. Bidding 2 of your suit here is a rescue bid which I will explain presently.

IF IT'S A MINOR SUIT, BID 2 NO TRUMP

If your five-card suit is a minor suit and you have 8 or 9 points, bid 2 No Trump.

As South you hold:

♠ K x x x   ♡ K J x x x   ◇ x x x   ♣ x

You have 9 points.

The bidding:

North *Opens* with *1 No Trump*. South *Responds 2 Clubs* and on the next round you bid your five-card Heart suit showing 8 or 9 points and a five-card suit.

♠ A K x x x   ♡ A x x x   ◇ x x x   ♣ x

The bidding:

North *Opens* with *1 No Trump*. Bid *3 Spades,* showing 10 points (or more) and a five-card Spade suit.

2 CLUB OR "STAYMAN CONVENTION"

Oh, yes, I haven't explained the 2 Club Convention yet, have I? This convention is more commonly called the Stayman Convention and can be very simple if you don't go out of your way to complicate it. It is one of the few artificial conventions that I recommend and is used by the responder when Partner has opened with a No Trump bid.

2 CLUB BID MERELY ASKS PARTNER
A QUESTION

The 2 Club response merely asks Partner a question, "Partner, do you have a four-card major suit? I have one, and if you have one also, I feel that the hand may play better in a major suit contract if we have eight trumps together. If my weak suit is your weak suit we may be in trouble at a No Trump contract."

MUST HAVE NO TRUMP TYPE HAND

The only thing you have to be concerned about is this: If Partner says "No," which is a 2 Diamond bid, then you will have to return the bid to No Trump. So, you must have a No Trump type hand to use the 2 Club bid.

HOW NO TRUMP OPENING BIDDER
ANSWERS QUESTION

The opening No Trump bidder will answer your question in the following manner:

If he has no four-card major suit he will bid 2 Diamonds.

If he has only a four-card Heart suit he will bid 2 Hearts.

If he has a four-card Spade suit he will bid 2 Spades.

Now, suppose he has both a four-card Spade suit and a four-card Heart suit. He will still bid 2 Spades.

Now, the question is: "How can your team arrive at a Heart contract when you are looking for a four-card Heart suit from the opening bidder and he bids 2 Spades even though he has four Hearts too?"

Let's say you have 10 points and a No Trump type hand. You would normally bid 3 No Trump; right? But, in this hand you have a worthless doubleton and a four-card Heart suit. So, you will bid 2 Clubs, asking Partner if he too has four Hearts to go with yours. If he bids 2 Diamonds, you will rebid 3 No Trump.

If he had bid 2 Hearts, then you would rebid 4 Hearts.

If he had bid 2 Spades, you would return to 3 No Trump because Partner missed your Heart suit; right? Partner now knows that your four-card major suit must have been Hearts. If he has four Hearts also, he will realize that the partnership has an eight-card suit in Hearts and he will return to 4 Hearts.

MAY USE 2 CLUB BID WITH 8 POINTS
OR 21 POINTS

If you had had 8 or 9 points, instead of 10, you would have returned the bidding to either 2 No Trump instead of 3 or to 3 Hearts or 3 Spades instead of 4.

If you had had 17 points you would have returned the bidding to 6 No Trump or you would have been interested in a 6 Heart or 6 Spade bid, whichever the case might be. In other words, you may use the 2 Club bid with any hand that contains 8 points or more. The bid is merely asking partner where the hand should be played, in a major suit or in No Trump.

Sample hands with which you would use the 2 Club Convention:

♠ A x x x   ♡ Q x x x   ◇ x x   ♣ K x x

♠ K Q x   ♡ K J x x   ◇ Q x x x   ♣ x x

♠ A K x x   ♡ Q J x   ◇ Q x x x   ♣ K Q

RESCUE BIDS

If you adopt this convention as part of your system, and all the better players are doing so, you have available to you the rescue bid. You, no doubt, have had partners open with 1 No Trump and found yourself with no points, yet you did have a long suit in your hand. At No Trump this suit is worthless, but played in a suit it would produce a number of tricks. So, you just bid 2 of the long suit, either 2 Spades, 2 Hearts or 2 Diamonds. This bid says, "Partner, I haven't any points, that is, seven or less, but I have a good suit." Partner, the opening bidder, must pass this bid unless he has the very top of his point count and four cards in your suit. If your long suit is Clubs you will have to bid 2 Clubs first and then return to 3 Clubs. Now, partner knows that you are interested in a Club suit rather than just asking for a major suit.

As South you hold:

♠ x   ♡ K x x x x x   ◇ x x x   ♣ x x x

The bidding:

North opens with 1 No Trump. Bid 2 Hearts, showing no points up to 7 points. A rescue bid.

THE GERBER "4 CLUB CONVENTION"

Sometimes you will want to know immediately after your partner has opened 1, 2 or 3 No Trump how many Aces he has. You have already learned that if you bid 4 No Trump, after a No Trump opening bid, that you are *"Pushing"* for him to bid more if he has additional points, so you couldn't be asking for his Aces, could you? In this event you should make an artificial bid of 4 Clubs. Your partner responds as follows:

4 Diamonds—Message, "I have no Aces."

4 Hearts—Message, "I have one Ace."

4 Spades—Message, "I have two Aces."

4 No Trump—Message, "I have three Aces."

4 Diamonds—Message, "I have four Aces."

If the 4 Club bidder wants to know about the Kings, he bids 5 Clubs and partner responds 5 Diamonds, 5 Hearts, etc., in the same manner as above.

EXAMPLE:

As South you hold:

♠ A x   ♡ A K J x x x x x   ◇ x x   ♣ x

North *Opens* with *1 No Trump*. Bid *4 Clubs* immediately. You are reasonably sure that your team has a Little Slam; however, if your opponents have the two missing Aces, you will lose two tricks, causing you to go down one. So you must find out how many Aces your partner has. (If you say *4 No Trump*, your partner will go to *6 No Trump* if he has 17 or 18 points and pass with only 16.) If he hasn't any Aces he will say *4 Diamonds* and you can sign off at *4 Hearts*.

OPENING WITH 19, 20 AND 21 POINTS
(NO TRUMP TYPE HANDS)

We have discussed this hand several times. These hands are opened with 1 of a suit and you jump in No Trump on your *Rebid*.

OPENING WITH 22, 23 AND 24 POINTS.
2 NO TRUMP HANDS

To open with *2 No Trump,* you must have the following requirements:

1. *All four suits* must be protected by guarded honors.

2. Your doubleton, if any, must be A x or K x. (Q x is not protected.)

3. Distribution same as *1 No Trump* opening bids, i.e.:

   a. No voids
   b. No singletons
   c. One doubleton at most

Rebids: Since you have practically given your partner a photostatic copy of your hand, there is no need for a *Rebid* unless you are *"Pushed."* Partner needs only 4 points to raise you. (Because your 22 points and his 4 points add up to 26.)

Responses to 2 No Trump Bids: If you can add and *"Push,"* you can handle the *Responses* to this bid. *Read* the *Responses to the 1 No Trump* bids. The same principle applies here.

OPENING WITH 25, 26, AND 27 POINTS.
3 NO TRUMP HANDS

Same requirements as the 2 No Trump hands.

SUMMARY

Opening Bid. (Hands with no voids or singletons, and at most one doubleton.)

1 No Trump, 16, 17 or 18 points. (*Three suits stopped. Doubleton must be Q x or better.*)

2 No Trump, 22, 23 or 24 points. (*All suits must be stopped.*)

3 No Trump, 25, 26 or 27 points. (*All suits must be stopped.*)

(With the 19-, 20- or 21-point hands you will open with 1 in a suit and jump in No Trump on your next bid.)

Responding with Balanced Hands. (No voids or singletons, and at most one doubleton.)

Just *ADD* your high-card points to Partner's minimum above promised points and if they add to:

26 points, *bid 3 No Trump*
33 points, *bid 6 No Trump*
37 points, *bid 7 No Trump*

HOWEVER, if partner needs 1 more point than the above minimum that he promised and your points add to ONLY:

25 points, *bid 2 No Trump*

32 points, *bid 4 No Trump*

37 points, *bid 5 No Trump*

RESPONDING WITH A BALANCED HAND WHICH CONTAINS A FOUR-CARD MAJOR SUIT

USE THE "2 CLUB CONVENTION" (called the Stayman Convention).

8 or 9 points or more (there is no upper limit).

Bid 2 Clubs, asking partner if he has a four-card major suit to go with yours.

RESPONSES TO THE "2 CLUB CONVENTION"

2 Diamonds says, "No, I do not have a four-card major suit."

2 Hearts says, "Yes, I have four Hearts, but I do not have four Spades."

2 Spades says, "Yes, I have four Spades, but I could also have four Hearts."

(When partner bids 2 Clubs looking for a four-card Heart suit from you and you bid 2 Spades, he will return to No Trump because you missed his suit. Now, you will know that his major suit had to be Hearts and you will then return the bidding to the Hearts suit.)

Responding with Unbalanced Hands. (Void, singleton or more than one doubleton.)

10 points or more with a five-card major suit, bid 3 of your suit. (If it is a five-card minor suit and 10 points, bid 3 No Trump immediately.)

8 or 9 points with a five-card major suit, bid 2 Clubs first and then bid your suit on the next round. (If it is a minor suit, bid 2 No Trump immediately.)

[88]

With 7 points or less and at least a six-card suit you may use the rescue bid and bid 2 Diamonds, 2 Hearts or 2 Spades because the hands will play better there than at partner's 1 No Trump. If your long suit is Clubs you will have to bid 2 Clubs and then bid 3 Clubs on the next round.

YOU MAY JUMP TO FOUR IN A MAJOR SUIT IF YOU HAVE A SIX-CARD SUIT AND LESS THAN 10 POINTS IN HIGH CARDS AND A SINGLETON OR A VOID.

QUIZ

In the following hands what is your opening bid?

1. ♠ A Q x   ♡ K x x   ◇ K Q x x   ♣ K x x

2. ♠ K J x   ♡ J x   ◇ K Q J x   ♣ A Q x x

3. ♠ A K Q x   ♡ Q x   ◇ x x x x   ♣ A Q x

4. ♠ A J x   ♡ K J   ◇ A Q J   ♣ A K J x x

5. ♠ A x   ♡ A Q J x   ◇ K Q x   ♣ K J x x

6. ♠ K Q J x   ♡ A Q   ◇ A K x x   ♣ K Q J

ANSWERS

1. You have 17 points. *Open* with *1 No Trump.*

2. You have 17 points. *Open* with *1 Diamond.* If you have a doubleton it must be Q x, K x, or A x to open with *1 No Trump.*

3. You have 17 points. The rule for opening *1 No Trump* is to have three suits guarded. Your Diamonds and Hearts are both unguarded. *Open* with *1 Club* and await developments.

4. You have 24 points. *Open* with *2 No Trump.*

5. You have 20 points. *Open* with *1 Heart* and *Jump* in *No Trump* on your rebid.

6. You have 25 points. *Open* with *3 No Trump.*

QUIZ

In the following hand you are South:

♠ K x x x   ♡ K J x x x   ◇ x x x   ♣ x

The bidding has gone:

North	South
1 No Trump	2 Clubs
2 Diamonds	2 Hearts

7. What message is South sending to North with his 2 Club bid?

8. What message is North sending to South with his 2 Diamond rebid?

9. What message is South sending to North when he rebids 2 Hearts?

ANSWERS

7. "Partner, do you have a four-card major?"

8. "Partner, I do not have a four-card major suit."

9. "Partner, when I bid my major suit after you denied having a four-card major, you know that it has to be a five-card suit; otherwise, I would have rebid 2 No Trump. I had an 'old-fashioned' 2 Heart response to your opening No Trump bid."

QUIZ

Suppose, with this same hand,

♠ K x x x   ♡ K J x x x   ◇ x x x   ♣ x

The bidding has gone:

North	South
1 No Trump	2 Clubs
2 Hearts	?

10. What would you rebid now?

ANSWERS

10. *4 Hearts.* You can't count on more than 16 points from North because you forced him to bid again when you employed the "2 Club Convention" but since he "hit" your suit, you can promote your singleton to 3 points. You will have 26 points, so you must bid the game.

QUIZ

In the following hands you are South. Your partner has opened the bidding with *1 No Trump*. What is your response?

11. ♠ A J 10 x x   ♡ K x x   ◇ Q x x x   ♣ x

12. ♠ x   ♡ K Q 10 x x x   ◇ x x x   ♣ J x x

13. ♠ A J x   ♡ K Q x x   ◇ Q J x   ♣ Q J x

ANSWERS

11. You have 12 points. *Respond* with *3 Spades.*

12. You have 6 points in high cards and a long major suit. *Bid 4 Hearts.*

13. *Bid 4 No Trump.* You have 16 points, and if your partner has more than the minimum of 16, you should have a *Slam* and you are "pushing" for him to bid it.

QUIZ

In the following hands you are South. Your partner has opened the bidding with *2 No Trump*. What is your response?

14. ♠ K x x x x   ♡ J x x   ◇ x x x x   ♣ x

15. ♠ Q x x   ♡ J x x   ◇ J x x x   ♣ x x x

16. ♠ K x x   ♡ Q x x   ◇ K Q x   ♣ x x x x

17. ♠ K Q x   ♡ A J x x   ◇ Q x x   ♣ Q x x

ANSWERS

14. *Bid 4 Spades.* Your partner promises 22 points and you have 6 with distribution so you must bid game.

15. *Bid 3 No Trump.* His 22 points and your 4 make 26 which is required for game in No Trump. His *2 No Trump* promises a stop in every suit.

16. *Bid 4 No Trump,* pushing him to go on to a *Little Slam* if he has more points than the minimum of 22 he promised.

17. *Bid 5 No Trump.* If your partner has the top of his bid (23 or 24 points), he should bid *7 No Trump* because you are pushing him. You could also bid the "Gerber 4 Club Convention" (see page 85) because you are close enough to *7 No Trump.* You have 14 points in high cards and your partner promised you 22 points. You have 36 points. There are only 4 points out against you. If the 4 points are an Ace, then you will not make 7. The "Gerber 4 Club Convention" asks your partner how many Aces he has. If he has the three missing Aces, go to 7. If not, stop at *6 No Trump.*

CHAPTER IX

Opening Suit Bids of 2, 3, 4 and 5

OVERCALLS AND COUNTING YOUR WINNERS

Before you can fully understand these bids, you must first be able to count your winners. The *Opening 2 Bid* promises within one trick of game in your hand when you open the bidding. The *Opening* bid of 3, 4 and 5 promises within two tricks *of the Bid* if you are vulnerable and within three tricks of the *Bid* if not vulnerable. The *Overcall* promises the same as the *3, 4* and *5* Bids but for a different reason. If you are unable to count winners in your hand, how can you tell whether the above situations exist or not?

You must also be able to understand defensive scoring. In the *3, 4* and *5 Bids*, you are deliberately taking a "set" to block the opponents' communication system. In the *Overcalls* you aren't deliberately taking a "set," but you are preparing yourself for a possible set if the trumps are stacked against you. Your right-hand opponent has already bid and your left-hand opponent could have most of your trumps. If you have a certain number of winners in your hand, you can't be hurt too badly even though the opponents *double*. (This will be explained in detail later.)

HOW TO COUNT YOUR WINNERS

A winner is a trick that you would normally expect to take in a hand. In the following hands how many tricks would you expect to take?

♠ A K Q x x   ♡ Q J 10 9 x x   ◇ x   ♣ x

You will expect to have nine winners if the hand is played at Spades or Hearts. In your Spade suit you would probably take five tricks: the A K Q and two long-card tricks that will probably set up. In your Heart suit you would expect to take four tricks. Your Queen and Jack will probably lose to the Ace and King, and your 10 and 9 will draw the other Hearts, and your two long-card tricks will set up. No winners in the Diamond and Club suits.

♠ J 10 9 8 7 6 5 4   ♡ A x   ◇ K Q x   ♣ None

You should have eight winners in this hand. There are eight cards in the Spade suit, so there are only five Spades in the other three hands. When you play the Jack, three Spades will probably fall on it, leaving only two Spades out. Lead the 10-spot and these cards will fall. You have lost these two tricks, but the next six long-card tricks will set up. You will take the Ace of Hearts and either the King or Queen of Diamonds.

♠ A K Q x x x   ♡ Q   ◇ A K Q x x   ♣ x

You should take six Spade tricks. None in Hearts. Five Diamond tricks and none in Clubs, giving you eleven winners.

♠ x   ♡ J 10 9 8 6 3   ◇ K Q J x   ♣ A x

You should have six winners. None in Spades. Three Heart tricks. Two Diamond tricks and one in Clubs.

♠ A J 8 7 6 5 3 2   ♡ x   ◇ x x x   ♣ x

You should take seven winners in Spades. When you play the Ace of Spades, you will probably draw three other cards of that suit, leaving only two out. The odds are that those two will fall on the Jack, which you will lose. The rest of your cards should set up as long-card tricks.

♠ Q J 9 8 7   ♡ K x   ◇ Q J 10 9   ♣ J x

You should have four winners. You should take at least two tricks in Spades. The Queen and Jack will lose to the Ace and King, and if the 9-spot loses to the 10-spot, your 8 and 7 will be good. You can't count the King of Hearts as a winner because it has only a 50-50 chance of taking a trick. You will have two winners in Diamonds and none in Clubs.

♠ K 10 9 3   ♡ x   ◇ x x   ♣ K Q J 7 6 3

You should have five winners in the hand. You can't count a trick in Spades unless you are the optimistic type. None in Hearts or Diamonds and five winners in Clubs. You will lose the King of Clubs to the Ace drawing three Clubs and leaving four Clubs in the other three hands. The Queen and Jack should draw them and set up your 7, 6 and 3 as long-card tricks.

♠ K 10 9 8 6 5   ♡ Q J 10 3   ◇ x x   ♣ x

You should have four winners in the hand. You should have three winners in Spades. The King will lose to the Ace. The 10- and 9-spots will probably lose to the Queen and Jack, and the 8 will draw in any other card that is still out, setting up the 6- and 5-spot. You will have one Heart trick. The Queen and Jack will probably lose to the Ace and King, and your 10-spot will be a good trick. None in Diamonds and Clubs.

♠ K Q J 10 9   ♡ x x x   ◇ Q x x   ♣ x x

Four winners in Spades. You will lose the King to the Ace and your next four cards will be good. None in the other three suits.

♠ A K Q J x x x   ♡ A x x   ◇ A x   ♣ x

You will have nine winners in the hand. You should have seven winners in Spades. One in Hearts and Diamonds, and none in Clubs.

♠ A K J   ♡ A K J x x   ◇ A   ♣ K Q 10 x

You should have eight winners in the hand. You should have two winners in Spades, at least four winners in Hearts, and one in Diamonds and one in Clubs.

♠ A K x x   ♡ A K x x   ◇ x   ♣ A K x x

You have 6 Quick Tricks. You can't count them as winners because you don't have a suit that you could call trumps without some support from your partner.

♠ Q J 10   ♡ A Q J x   ◇ x x x   ♣ A x x

You should have one trick in Spades, two in Hearts, none in Diamonds and one in Clubs. Your Heart suit is rather weak to think of putting in a bid and expecting it to be trumps without help from your partner.

♠ Q x   ♥ K J 10 x x x   ♦ K J x x x   ♣ None

You should expect to have six winners in the hand. None in Spades. You should take four tricks in the Heart suit. Your King will lose to the Ace; this will draw three Hearts leaving four Hearts out in the other three hands. Your Jack will lose to the Queen bringing three more Hearts, leaving only one more Heart out which you will take with your good 10-spot. Your three small cards will set up as long-card tricks. In your Diamond suit you should expect to take two tricks. Your King will lose to the Ace. Your Jack will lose to the Queen. Your first small card will probably lose to the 10- or 9-spot, and by this time the last two small cards should set up as long-card tricks. None in Clubs.

♠ K x x x x   ♥ x x x   ♦ A K Q   ♣ x x

You have only three tricks in Diamonds and two tricks in Spades. You haven't a suit to bid so you can't open this hand.

♠ x   ♥ A Q J x   ♦ K J x x x   ♣ A K x

This hand should have five or six winners. None in Spades. Two in Hearts. You will take the Ace and your Queen will probably lose to the King and your Jack will set up. May I explain here that the only way your fourth small card can set up is for all of the other three players to have three cards each, which isn't too common. The fourth card will set up as a long-card trick quite frequently when you have a five- or six-card suit but not when you have just a four-card suit. You should take one or (to add up as above) two Diamond tricks and two Club tricks.

♠ K x   ♥ A x x   ♦ A J 10 x x   ♣ K J x

You have possibly four winners in the hand. None in Spades. One in Hearts. Possibly three in Diamonds and none in Clubs.

In some hands your number of winners may depend on your own attitude toward the game. If you are a cautious player, you may not want to count some of the possible winners. This is another example of using your own reasoning power rather than a set of rules.

OPENING 2 BIDS (IN A SUIT)

(A Grownup Hand)

The Opening 2 Bid in a Suit is a very big hand. (The strongest bid that can be made.) *It promises your partner within one trick of game. It also promises your partner 4 Quick Tricks for a possible defensive play later. Your hand will have 21 points or more, unless you have a very long suit or have more than one biddable suit.*

Example:

♠ A K Q J x x x   ♡ A x x   ◇ A x   ♣ x

This hand has nine winners. Seven in Spades, one in Diamonds and one in Hearts. It takes ten tricks to make a game in Spades, so you would have a *2 Spade* opening bid (but not a *2 Club* or *2 Diamond* bid because it takes eleven tricks to make a game in a minor suit).

♠ A K Q J x x   ♡ Q J 10 9 8   ◇ x   ♣ x

This hand does not have as many points as the above hand but still will produce nine tricks which is one trick short of a game in Spades, but does it have 4 Quick Tricks? Your bid would be *1 Spade* and you would do something spectacular on your *rebid*.

The formula for opening the 2 (*Demand*) *Bid* is this:

With a five-card suit you need 25 points.

With a six-card suit you need 23 points.

With a seven-card suit you need 21 points.

If you have two five-card suits, deduct a point.

This is for a major suit. For a minor suit add 2 points to the above figures.

This formula is for those students who can't figure out winners and who like to do memory work. If you use the above formula, you are still supposed to be within one trick of game in your hand, however, and most of the time you will be.

[97]

RESPONDING TO A 2 DEMAND BID

Your partner has sent you a message saying: 'Partner, I have within one trick of game in my hand; you must keep the bidding open until a game is reached or unless our opponents have been doubled." Let me remind you that if a six-year-old can come along with a Junior High hand, he certainly could come along with a *Grownup Hand*; however, when he's with a grownup, he has to be on his best behavior or suffer the consequences, which will be in the form of a quick trick. *You* must have the trick that partner doesn't have. If a six- or seven-year-old doesn't have his Quick Trick, then he can't come along; it will take and eight- or nine-year-old provided he has just a half of a Quick Trick. If these situations do not exist, then the *Responder must* bid 2 No Trump.

Suppose you hold the following hand and your partner has *opened* the bidding with *2 Spades:*

♠ Q x x x   ♡ A K Q x x x   ◇ x   ♣ x x

You will be tempted to *Respond* with *3 Hearts*. This is wrong. Always bid *3 Spades*.

Message:

"Partner, I have a positive *Response*. We may have a slam. I want to relieve your mind *immediately* by letting you know that we have a suit fit together. When I bid again, I will be showing you my Aces." This Heart suit will be perfect as a side suit for your partner on which to throw his losers.

Suppose you hold:

♠ x x   ♡ Q J x x x x   ◇ J x x   ♣ x x

Your partner opens with *2 Spades*. Your response will be *2 No Trump.*

Message:

"Partner, I don't have 6 or 7 points with a Quick Trick or 8 or 9 points with ½ Quick Trick."

Suppose the *Opening 2 Spades* bidder now says *3 Clubs?* You will now say *3 Hearts*.

Message:

"Partner, I didn't manufacture any points; I am obligated to keep bidding until we get to a game, and I can't raise your Spades or Clubs, but I have a suit of my own that maybe *you* can support or maybe we can play the contract at *No Trump.*"

Suppose you hold:

♠ x x   ♡ x x x x   ◇ x x x x   ♣ x x x

Oh, yes, it's possible. After you have said *2 No Trump* to an *opening 2 Spade* bid and partner *Rebids 3 Clubs*, just say *3 No. Trump.*

Message:

"Partner, I meant business when I said *2 No Trump*. I don't have support for either suit you have bid. I don't have a suit of my own. I don't have any points. I just don't have nothin'! You have forced me to keep bidding until a game has been reached, and *3 No Trump* is game. I have fulfilled my obligation."

OPENING 3, 4 AND 5 BIDS (IN A SUIT)

When you open a suit bid of 3, 4 or 5, you are saying, "Partner, I am deliberately overbidding. I have heard of a rule called 'the Rule of 2 and 3,' which means: If our side is vulnerable, I'm only going set two tricks; but if our side is not vulnerable, I plan to go set three tricks. Don't raise me unless you can take care of my overbid tricks *plus* one more." Now the big question that many bridge players don't understand is: "Why would anyone in his right mind want to deliberately overbid and give points to his opponents?"

To answer this you must understand a number of things:

1. These bids are made on hands that have little defensive value. If you have your share of the high-card points in the deck, you *won't*

want to make a "sacrifice" bid. (Your share of points is 10 because there are 40 in the entire deck.)

2. You must have long suits which contain a certain number of winners.

3. If you have less than your share of high-card points in the deck and your partner has none at all with which to help you, then who has all of the points? Your opponents. Right? If they have this many points, won't they get lots of score anyway? They probably have a slam.

May I ask you a question? If you open the bidding with 3, 4, or 5 Spades, won't it be more difficult for your opponents to get to a game or a slam now? Haven't you fouled up their communicative system?

The 3, 4, and 5 bids are called "block bids" or "pre-emptive bids." They are designed to block the opponents from their normal method of transferring messages to each other.

When a bridge team makes a game, his opponents lose an average of 500 points. If the opponent chooses to overbid two tricks vulnerable and he is doubled, he loses 500 points. If he chooses to overbid three tricks not vulnerable and he is doubled, he still loses 500 points. So if he took the "sacrifice" rather than allowing the team to make a game, he has come out even. Right? Suppose, however, his opponents forgot to double, then he loses only 200 points if he's vulnerable, and 150 points if he isn't vulnerable, and he has come out ahead. If, however, he takes the set and blocks out a slam bid, then he has come out far ahead.

If you go set more than 500 points, you have made a bad block bid.

Block bids are made on the number of winners you have in your hand rather than points. You must study the opening section of this chapter on "How to Count Your Winners" before you use the "Rule of 2 and 3." I have played with players who will open with a 3 bid on the fourth hand. After both of your opponents have had an opportunity to bid, are you blocking their communicative system? Absolutely not. If you overbid now, you are just handing your opponents points on a silver platter.

PARTNER OF THE OPENING 3, 4 AND 5 BIDDER

If your side is vulnerable, you must have the two tricks your partner is expecting to go "set" plus the additional trick or tricks that you bid.

If not vulnerable you must have the three tricks plus your additional bid. Bid the full value of your hand on your first bid.

OVERCALLS

When a player *Overcalls* or makes a bid after his opponent has bid, he is saying, "Partner, you can't depend on my having an *Opening Bid*. I am bidding the 'Rule of 2 and 3.' If our side is vulnerable, I won't go down but two tricks. If not vulnerable I won't go down but three tricks. This isn't a 'block bid' but I have to protect myself against my left-hand opponent having six of my suit 'bunched' in his hand. If they are, he will surely double me because his partner *opened* the bidding, sending a message that he had at least 13 points in his hand."

Again you must learn to count winners before you can bid the "Rule of 2 and 3."

PARTNER OF THE OVERCALLER

If an *Overcall* sends out the above message, then as the partner of the *Overcaller* you will have to *Respond* differently. You can raise with less trump support because he should have a five-card suit to overcall. You will be more reluctant to naming your own suit and try to raise your partner's suit when possible. Remember that the overcaller is not obligated to bid again and may leave you in *your suit*. You should name your own suit only if you could have overcalled independently of your partner. There is no need to answer an overcall unless you feel that a game is in sight. As the partner of an overcaller you must also be able to count winners.

Since he suggests to you that he may go set two tricks if your side is vulnerable and three tricks if your side is not vulnerable, then you should have those additional tricks plus another one if you bid again.

As the partner of the overcaller, you can be more liberal in counting winners.

Your partner promised you a few high cards when he overcalled, so you can now count K x as a possible trick. You will hope that one of his high cards is the Ace or Queen of that suit.

Example:

As East your side is vulnerable and you hold:

♠ A K 9 4   ♡ 9 7 2   ◇ 10 4 2   ♣ K 8 7

The bidding:

South	West	North	East
1 Diamond	1 Heart	Pass	?

West has promised to take five tricks. You should be able to take three tricks (two Spade tricks and a possible Club trick) which will give you eight tricks and a 2 Heart bid. If West had additional tricks, he will go on.

As East your side is vulnerable and you hold:

♠ x   ♡ K 10 7 4   ◇ Q 9 7 3   ♣ A 10 5 3

The bidding:

South	West	North	East
1 Diamond	1 Heart	Pass	?

West has promised five tricks. You should be able to take two Heart tricks, one Diamond trick, and one Club trick, making nine tricks which is a *3 Heart* bid so you should bid it. (When responding to overcalls and pre-emptive bids, you should show the full value of your hand in one bid.)

You should have at least 10 points to respond to an overcall.

JUMP OVERCALLS

A *Jump Overcall* is treated in the same manner as the "Opening 3, 4 or 5 Bids." If your right-hand opponent opens the bidding with *1 Club* and you hold:

♠ Q J 10 9 x x x   ♡ x x   ◇ K Q x   ♣ x

Your hand looks rather hopeless from a defensive standpoint because your opponents will probably be trumping Spades before you set up a trick. You have only one probable defensive trick in your hand, the King or Queen of Diamonds. If your partner hasn't any points, the opponents should at least have a game. You should bid *3 Spades* if you aren't vulnerable. You will expect to take five tricks in Spades (if Spades are trumps) and one in Diamonds, giving you six tricks. You have contracted to take nine tricks when you bid *3 Spades*. If you are doubled and partner can't help you at all, you will lose 500 points. Just remember that you would have lost that many points anyway if your opponents had bid and made a game, or even more if they had bid and made a slam.

In the following hand you hold:

♠ Q J 10 9 x x x x   ♡ x   ◇ K Q x   ♣ x

Your hand looks even more hopeless from a defensive standpoint. Your opponents will certainly be trumping Spades in a hurry, but you have one more trump than before if Spades are trumps so open with *4 Spades* instead of 3. This will certainly foul up their communication system.

PARTNER OF THE JUMP OVERCALLER

Same as "Partner of the Opening 3, 4 or 5 Bidder."

QUIZ

In the following hands, your side is not vulnerable. What are your opening bids?

1. ♠ Q 10 9 8 7 6 5 4   ♡ A 5   ◇ K Q 8   ♣ None
2. ♠ A K Q x x x   ♡ Q   ◇ A K Q x x   ♣ x
3. ♠ A J 8 7 6 5 3 2   ♡ x   ◇ x x x   ♣ x
4. ♠ J 10 9 7 5 4 2   ♡ 10 4 3   ◇ x x   ♣ A

ANSWERS

1. *Bid 1 Spade.* Your hand is too strong for a block bid because you have your share of high-card points (11). Your side may have the game instead of the opponents.

2. *Bid 2 Spades*. You have eleven winners. You needed only nine. A bid of two in a suit is the strongest bid you can make.

3. *Bid 4 Spades*. Your hand is almost worthless as a defensive hand, but you have seven winners if Spades are trumps. If your partner can't help you, and you go set your three tricks "doubled," you will lose 500 points. If your partner doesn't have any high cards, then who has them? Your opponents, and they, no doubt, have a slam. If you don't block their communication system, then you will lose 700 to 1000 points or more, so 4 Spades is a good bid. If your partner has a good hand, then you haven't lost anything. You just make your bid. Right?

4. *Bid 3 Spades,* since you aren't vulnerable. The Spade suit should produce five tricks unless the distribution is unusual, and the Ace of Clubs should produce the sixth trick. You have contracted to take nine tricks when you bid *3 Spades*. However, you are telling your partner that you will go set three tricks.

QUIZ

In the following hands, your side is not vulnerable. Your right-hand opponent opened with *1 Heart*. What is your bid?

5. ♠ A J 8 7 6 5 3 2   ♡ x   ♢ x x x   ♣ x

6. ♠ Q J 9 8 7   ♡ K x   ♢ Q J 10 9   ♣ J x

7. ♠ K J 9 7 5   ♡ K x x   ♢ K J 9   ♣ A Q

Would you *Overcall* with *1 Spade?*

ANSWERS

5. *Bid 4 Spades*. See answer to #3 (same hand). Jump overcall.

6. *Bid 1 Spade*. You have contracted to take seven tricks. You have four tricks no matter how many points your opponents have. You are bidding the "Rule of 2 and 3."

7. No. Even though you have more points than the above hand, you do not have as good a hand for *Overcalling*. If your left-

hand opponent has the A Q 10 8 6 of Spades, you haven't a single Spade trick. You can't count on a Heart trick. You have only one Diamond trick and only one Club trick. Many players will *Overcall 1 Spade* with this hand, and if they have "sharp" opponents, they may be doubled and can go set 1400 points or more. This is a hand for a "Take-out double" (next lesson).

QUIZ

8. As South you hold:

   ♠ J 9 4 3　　♡ 9 8　　◇ 5 4 3　　♣ J 8 6 2

   North *Opens* with *2 Spades*. What is your *Response?*

9. As South you hold:

   ♠ J 9　　♡ K Q 7　　◇ J 9 7 4　　♣ Q 5 3 2

   North *Opens* with *2 Spades*. What is your *Response?*

10. As South you hold:

    ♠ J 5 4 3　　♡ A K Q 7 5　　◇ 10 3　　♣ 9 7

    North *Opens* with *2 Spades*. What is your *Response?*

11. As South your side is vulnerable and you hold:

    ♠ J 8 7　　♡ K 9　　◇ K Q 7 6　　♣ A 8 6 4

    The bidding:

West	North	East	South
1 Diamond	1 Heart	2 Diamonds	?

    What is your *Response?*

12. As South your side is vulnerable and you hold:

    ♠ 8 7 4 3　　♡ 9 2　　◇ A K 4　　♣ J 8 4 2

    The bidding:

West	North	East	South
1 Diamond	1 Heart	Pass	?

    What is your *Response?*

ANSWERS

8. *Bid 2 No Trump.* Message: "Partner, I do not have the 6 points and 1 Quick Trick that is necessary to raise you." If North should *Rebid* another suit, you will then raise his Spades.

[105]

9. *Bid 3 No Trump*. You have 9 points and 1 Quick Trick. You must give a positive *Response*. You can't raise your partner's suit with only J 9, and you don't have a suit of your own to name. If you *Respond* with *2 No Trump*, you are denying your Point Count so you must respond *3 No Trump*.

10. *Bid 3 Spades*. You will be tempted to name your Heart suit, but let your partner know immediately that you have a suit fit. Any suit you bid later will be showing Aces. This enables you to reach slams.

11. *Bid 2 Hearts*. North has promised you five tricks and a good Heart suit when he *Overcalled*. You should produce one Heart trick, one Diamond trick, and one Club trick, making eight tricks and a *2 Heart* bid.

12. Pass. Some players would bid *1 No Trump* to show a guarded honor in Diamonds. Your partner promises five tricks; he has made a contract to take seven tricks. You have his two tricks that he needs to make his bid, so let well enough alone and pass. If you had one more trick, maybe in Clubs, you could bid 1 No Trump because you would have a desire to go on.

CHAPTER X

The Take-Out Double

The *Take-Out Double* is a double made after an opponent has bid. The message the double sends is: "Partner, I have the point-count requirement for an *Opening Bid* (13 points). I can support any suit that you bid or else I have a suit of my own to bid later. If I *Overcall*, I'm showing you a weaker hand and besides I may get into trouble if my suit has skips in it."

Before you can learn when to make a *Take-Out Double*, you must first be able to distinguish between a *Take-Out Double* and a *Penalty Double*. A *Penalty Double* is a double saying, "Partner, I don't believe our opponents can fulfill their contract. If I double and they go down, we will make a better score than if we play the hand." A *Take-Out Double* is a double asking partner to name his best suit.

To recognize a Take-Out Double the following requirements are necessary:

1. You must *Double* at your first opportunity to *Double*.

2. You must *Double* before your partner has made a bid.

3. You must have support for any suit that your partner might bid *or* you must have a suit of your own to bid later.

4. The *Doubled* bid must be at the level of one, two, or three in order to be considered a *Take-Out Double*.

1. You must *Double* at the first opportunity to *Double*.

You are South:

South	West	North	East
Pass	Pass	Pass	1 Diamond
Double			

When South passed the first time, he couldn't double because no one had bid. You may wonder how a player can make a *Take-Out Double* but cannot *Open the Bidding*. Let's examine the following hand.

♠ x x   ♡ A J x x   ◇ K J x x   ♣ Q J x

You have 13 points but only 1½ Quick Tricks. After your opponents bid *1 Spade*, you can support any suit that your partner names. He will know that you were just short of an opening bid. It's possible that your side can play the hand for a part score.

2. You must *Double* before your partner has made a bid.

You are North:

South	West	North	East
1 Heart	1 Spade	*Double*	Pass

One of the reasons for making a *Take-Out Double* is to find your partner's best suit. Obviously his best suit is Hearts because that is the suit he bid. So this has to be a *Penalty Double*.

3. You must have support for any suit that your partner might bid *or* you must have a suit of your own to bid later.

As South you hold:

♠ A Q x x   ♡ x   ◇ A J x x   ♣ A x x x

East *Opens* with *1 Heart*.

What do you do?

Double.

Message:

"Partner, I can support your Spades, Diamonds or Clubs or I have a suit of my own to bid later, and I have at least 13 points."

[108]

Many bridge players will want to overcall on this hand. Let's examine the hazards of this bid. First your partner will not realize that you have 17 points and you may miss a game. Second, suppose you *Overcall* with *1 Spade* (your best suit) and your left-hand opponent is sitting there with K J 10 9 8 and 7 of your suit and the King and Queen of Diamonds, you will take only three tricks, going set four tricks. This is quite possible. You must be prepared, when you *Overcall*, to be sitting between two good hands. You know that you have one on your right because he opened the bidding.

As South you hold:

♠ A K Q x x   ♡ x x x   ◇ x   ♣ A J x x

East opens with *1 Heart*.

What do you do?

Double.

Message:

(Same as above only this time you have a suit of your own to bid later. You could *Overcall* with this hand and not be in any trouble, but you may miss a game because your partner will think that you have a weaker hand than 16 points.) After your partner has responded with *2 Diamonds*, which is probably what he will do since it is your shortest suit, you will name your Spade suit. Of course your partner will then know that you had a Spade suit of your own to bid.

Let's re-examine one of the above hands:

♠ A Q x x   ♡ x   ◇ A J x x   ♣ A x x x

You have 17 points. You feel that you *must* bid with this hand. Let's assume, however, that before you get a chance to bid your right-hand opponent bids *1 Spade* instead of a heart. What do you do? It would be too dangerous to *Overcall* with *2 Diamonds* because your suit isn't good enough. If you *Double* your partner will probably respond with *2 Hearts* and you won't have a convenient *Rebid*. You must pass hoping the opponents will get too high and you can *Double for Penalties*.

4. The *Doubled* bid must be at the level of one, two or three in order to be considered a *Take-Out Double*.

The question that is probably in your mind now is: How can you make a *Take-Out Double* when your opponents have opened the bidding with a 4 bid?

As you know, the opening 4 bid is made on a hand that is weak in high cards and is made to try and block the opponents' communication system. Suppose you are the opponent.

You are South:

♠ x   ♡ A K Q x   ♢ K J 10 x   ♣ A K J x

East has just opened with *4 Spades*. What do you do? If you double, your partner will think you are doubling for penalties and will leave it in, but you would rather play the hand yourself. You should bid *4 No Trump*. This is a "Super duper" *Take-Out Double*.

There are four players involved in a *Take-Out Double Situation*. Let's assume that North is the dealer and *Opening Bidder:*

1. *North: Opening Bidder*
2. *East: Take-Out Doubler*
3. *South: Partner of the Opening Bidder after a Take-Out Double*
4. *West: Partner of the Take-Out Doubler*

Let's take each one and see what their messages are as they *Bid* and *Rebid*.

OPENING BIDDER

When any player opens the bidding in 1 of a suit, he promises from 13 to approximately 21 points, 2 Quick Tricks, and a *Rebid*.

As the *Opening Bidder* if your partner *Redoubles*, then you must pass when it comes time to *Rebid*. Regardless of the bid made by the opponents, the *Redoubler* has the next opportunity to bid on your team. Give him a chance to describe his hand to you. At this point he has only said, "Partner, I have 11 points. I haven't told you *where* those points are."

TAKE-OUT DOUBLER

I have discussed in detail the requirements for the *Take-Out Doubler*. I will now give you the Point-Count requirements for *Rebidding*. Here is a simple formula:

As the *Take-Out Doubler:*

Your first bid shows.....................13 points or more

Your *Rebid* at the two level shows........from 16 to 18 points
(High School hand)

(In other words if you speak again you must have 16 points.)

Your *Rebid* at the three level shows........from 19 to 21 points
(College hand)

Your Rebid at the four level shows...........22 points or more
(Grownup hand)

PARTNER OF THE OPENING BIDDER AFTER A TAKE-OUT DOUBLE

11 points or more.............................*Redouble*

7, 8, 9 or 10 points.............(1) *Bid* a suit of your own;
(2) *Double raise* in your partner's suit

6 points or less.............*Raise* your partner's suit or *pass*

Let's discuss these bids more thoroughly!

11 Points or more—Redouble. This is the strongest bid you can make. One Spade doubled and redoubled will add up to 4 Spades, which is a game. If you make overtricks, each one of these will add an extra 100 or 200 points to your score, so you will enjoy playing a 1 bid *Doubled* and *Redoubled*.

After you have *Redoubled*, you are in the "driver's seat" and should be given the next opportunity to bid on your team. If the opponents bid and take you out of the *Redouble*, you will want to describe your hand to your partner before he bids again. Up to this point you have only told him that you have 11 points. You haven't told him where those points are as yet.

7, 8, 9 or 10 points—(1). *Bid* a suit of your own. If you have a suit of your own, you had better bid it now or you may never get a chance to later. This is a hand in the medium range.

EXAMPLE

You hold:

♠ x x   ♡ Q x x   ◊ A J x x x   ♣ J x x

Your partner *Opened* the bidding with *1 Spade.* Your right-hand opponent makes a *Take-Out Double.* What do you do? Bid *2 Diamonds.*

Message:

"Partner, I have a medium hand with a suit of my own. If I don't mention my suit now, the bidding may be so high later that I won't be able to show it. You know that I don't have 11 points or I *would have Redoubled.*

(2). *Double raise* in your partner's suit.

EXAMPLE

You hold:

♠ J x x x   ♡ Q x x   ◊ A J x x   ♣ x x

Your partner *Opened* the bidding with *1 Spade.* Your right hand opponent makes a *Take-Out Double.* What do you do? You have 10 points, and you jump in your partner's suit bidding *3 Spades.*

Message:

"Partner, I have from 7 to 10 points and good trump support. I'm deliberately trying to block our opponents' communication system. You know that I would have *Redoubled* if I had had 11 points."

6 points or less—*Raise* your partner's suit or *pass.*

EXAMPLE

You hold:

♠ J x x x   ♡ x x x   ◊ Q x x x   ♣ x x

Your partner *Opened* the bidding with *1 Spade*. Your right-hand opponent makes a *Take-Out Double*. What do you do? Raise to *2 Spades*.

Message:

"Partner, I'm just letting you know that I can support your suit so that if you want to take a sacrifice bid later you will know that we have a suit fit together. If I had had 11 points, I would have *Redoubled*. If I had had 7 to 10 points, I would have jumped in your suit, so I must have 6 points or less. Right?"

You hold:

♠ x x   ♡ x x x   ◊ Q J x x   ♣ Q x x x

Your partner *Opened* the bidding with *1 Spade*. Your right-hand opponent makes a *Take-Out Double*. What do you do? Pass.

Message:

"Partner, my hand just isn't good for anything."

PARTNER OF THE TAKE-OUT DOUBLER

There are only two situations where the *Partner of the Take-Out Doubler* can pass:

1. When your right-hand opponent has put in a bid. (An intervening bid.)
2. When you feel that your team can "set" the opponents' *Doubled* contract.

Since you are obligated to bid (if there has been no intervening bid), it is sometimes difficult to let your partner know how many points you have until you *Rebid*. If you pass on the *Rebid*, your partner who made the *Take-Out Double* will know that you had less than 6 points. If you bid again, he will know that you had from 7 to 10 points. How will he know if you have 11 points? You must bid one more than is necessary at your first bid. This you will do whether there has been an intervening bid or not. Here is a simple formula that I have worked out that gives you a complete story of the actions by the *Partner of the Take-Out Doubler:*

BIDDING WITHOUT AN INTERVENING BID	BIDDING AFTER AN INTERVENING BID
With 11 points—Jump in your suit or jump in No Trump.	Same.
With 8, 9 or 10 points (and the opponents' suit stopped)—Bid *1 No Trump.*	Same.
With 7, 8, 9 or 10 points (without a stop in the opponents suit). —Bid your best suit. Listen to partner's next bid and add your points to his and bid accordingly.	Same. (You will show these points immediately because there has been an intervening bid.)

If the opponents *Redouble,* you just treat it as if there were no intervening bid. Name your best suit. However, if according to your hand, it doesn't matter which suit the hand is played in, just pass and let the *Doubler* select the suit.

With 11 Points—Jump in your suit or jump in No Trump. This bid is the same whether you have an intervening bid or not.

You hold:

♠ J x x   ♡ K J x x   ♢ K Q x   ♣ Q x x

Your partner has just *Doubled 1 Spade.* What is your bid? *3 Hearts.*

Message:

"Partner, I have at least 11 points and my best suit is Hearts."

Or you hold:

♠ K J x   ♡ Q J x   ♢ Q J x x   ♣ Q x x

2 No Trump.

Message:

"Partner, I have at least 11 points and a good stop in the opponents' suit."

With 8, 9 or 10 points (and the opponents' suit stopped)—Bid *1 No Trump*.

You hold:

♠ K J x x   ♡ J x x   ◇ Q x x   ♣ Q x x

Your partner has just *Doubled a 1 Spade* bid. What is your response? *1 No Trump*.

Message:

"Partner, I have 8, 9 or 10 points and the Spade suit stopped. If I had 11 points, I would have jumped in No Trump. I would have bid the same even if my right-hand opponent had put in a bid."

With 7, 8, 9 or 10 points (without a stop in the opponents' suit)—Bid your best suit.

You hold:

♠ x x   ♡ K x x x x   ◇ Q J x   ♣ J x x

Your partner has *Doubled* a *1 Spade* bid. What do you bid? *2 Hearts*.

Message if there is no intervening bid:

"Partner, I have made my bid, and Hearts is my best suit. I may have absolutely no points or I may have 10 points. If I had 11 points, I would have jumped in Hearts. The only way you can tell whether I have a legitimate bid is when I rebid. If I get a chance, I will bid again showing you 7, 8, 9 or 10 points."

Message after an intervening bid:

"Partner, I didn't have to bid so now that I have bid I show you 7, 8, 9 or 10 points. If I had had 11 points, I would have jumped and with less than 7 points, I would have passed."

EXAMPLES

You hold:

♠ x x x x   ♡ x x x   ◇ x x x   ♣ x x x

Suppose your partner has just *Doubled 1 Spade.* Your right-hand opponent has bid *2 Diamonds.* What do you do? Pass. The *2 Diamonds* bid made by your right-hand opponent has just relieved you of your obligation. Now your partner knows that you have 6 points or less. (Partner must double again if he still insists on knowing your best suit.)

Suppose, however, that your right-hand opponent passed. Now what do you do? You must bid. Right? Do you think that you can "set" the opponents? Absolutely not. You must bid your three-card Club suit. (The cheapest bid you can make.) Yes, this happens occasionally. Don't worry about it; your partner asked for it.

The *Opening Bidder* can make a *Take-Out Double* on *his Rebid.* After you have opened the bidding and your partner fails to say anything, you can *Double* your opponents on your *Rebid* to insist that your partner bid.

For example you are South:

The bidding:

South	West	North	East
1 Heart	*1 Spade*	Pass	Pass
Double			

Message:

"Partner, please bid your best suit. I have a beautiful hand, but I want to know the best place to play it." *Opener's* hand could be as follows:

♠ x x   ♡ A K J x   ◇ K Q J x   ♣ A Q J

or:

♠ x   ♡ A K x x   ◇ K J x x   ♣ A J x x

Your partner must respond in the same manner as to any *Take-Out Double.*

THE TAKE-OUT DOUBLE CHART

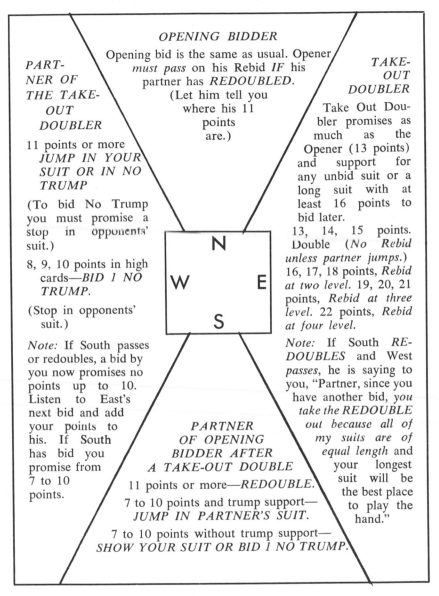

OPENING BIDDER

Opening bid is the same as usual. Opener *must pass* on his Rebid *IF* his partner has *REDOUBLED.* (Let him tell you where his 11 points are.)

PART-NER OF THE TAKE-OUT DOUBLER

11 points or more *JUMP IN YOUR SUIT OR IN NO TRUMP*

(To bid No Trump you must promise a stop in opponents' suit.)

8, 9, 10 points in high cards—*BID 1 NO TRUMP.*

(Stop in opponents' suit.)

Note: If South passes or redoubles, a bid by you now promises no points up to 10. Listen to East's next bid and add your points to his. If South has bid you promise from 7 to 10 points.

TAKE-OUT DOUBLER

Take Out Doubler promises as much as the Opener (13 points) and support for any unbid suit or a long suit with at least 16 points to bid later.

13, 14, 15 points. Double (*No Rebid unless partner jumps.*) 16, 17, 18 points, *Rebid at two level.* 19, 20, 21 points, *Rebid at three level.* 22 points, *Rebid at four level.*

Note: If South *RE-DOUBLES* and West *passes,* he is saying to you, "Partner, since you have another bid, *you take the REDOUBLE out because all of my suits are of equal length* and your longest suit will be the best place to play the hand."

PARTNER OF OPENING BIDDER AFTER A TAKE-OUT DOUBLE

11 points or more—*REDOUBLE.*

7 to 10 points and trump support— *JUMP IN PARTNER'S SUIT.*

7 to 10 points without trump support— *SHOW YOUR SUIT OR BID 1 NO TRUMP.*

QUIZ

Your right-hand opponent has opened the bidding with *1 Spade*. You are holding the following hands. What do you do?

1. ♠ x x   ♡ A J x   ◇ K J x x   ♣ A K x x

2. ♠ K x x   ♡ A x x   ◇ A K J x x x   ♣ x

3. ♠ A Q 10 8 4   ♡ x   ◇ x x x x   ♣ A K x

4. Suppose, however, with hand #3, your right-hand opponent opens the bidding with *1 Heart*. Now what is your bid?

ANSWERS

1. *Double.* You can support Hearts, Diamonds, or Clubs. You have 17 points.

2. *Double.* Your partner will probably bid *2 Clubs* because that is your shortest suit. You can then bid *2 Diamonds*. (You have a suit of your own to bid later.) You have 17 points.

3. *Pass.* If you double, your partner will have to consider it a *Take-Out Double* and you can't support any suit he bids and you don't have a suit of your own to bid. You must wait, and if they bid again, you can double for penalties. You have 15 points.

4. *Double.* You can support any suit that partner might bid.

QUIZ

In the following hands, you are South. North opens with *1 Spade*. East doubles. What is your response?

5. ♠ J x x x   ♡ K J x x   ◇ K Q x x   ♣ x

6. ♠ x x   ♡ A Q x x x   ◇ Q x x   ♣ x x x

7. ♠ x x x x   ♡ J x x x   ◇ K x x   ♣ J x

8. ♠ x x x   ♡ J x x x   ◇ K x x   ♣ J x x

ANSWERS

5. *Redouble.* You have more than 11 points. (14 in support of Spades.)

6. *Bid 2 Hearts.* You have a medium hand (9 points) and if you don't mention your suit now, you probably won't get a chance to mention it later.

7. *Bid 2 Spades.* You have trump support for your partner. This is about all this bid promises. You have 5 points.

8. *Pass.* A hand with less than 6 points and no trump support should be passed. You have 5 points.

QUIZ

In the following hands, your partner has doubled an opponent's bid of *1 Club.* Your right-hand opponent has passed. What is your response?

9. ♠ x x x   ♡ Q x x x   ◇ x x x   ♣ K x x

10. ♠ K Q x   ♡ K J x x x   ◇ Q x x   ♣ x x

11. ♠ K x x   ♡ Q J x   ◇ Q x x x   ♣ K J x

12. ♠ K x x x x   ♡ x   ◇ A x   ♣ Q J 10 x x

13. ♠ x x x   ♡ x x x   ◇ x x x   ♣ x x x x

ANSWERS

9. *Bid 1 Heart.* You have been forced to bid and your best suit is Hearts. After an intervening bid, you would pass. You have only 5 points.

10. *Bid 2 Hearts,* one more than is necessary because you have 11 points or more. (You have 12 points.)

11. *Bid 2 No Trump.* You have 11 points or more (12 points). You must jump in No Trump.

12. *Pass.* You can probably set the opponents.

13. *Bid 1 Diamond.* Your only four-card suit is the one your opponent has bid and you can't pass because you don't think you can set his *1 Club* bid. A Diamond is the cheapest bid you can make.

QUIZ

In the following hands, you are East and the bidding has gone:

South	West	North	East
1 Diamond	Double	Redouble	?

What are your responses when you hold the following:

14. ♠ J x x   ♡ x x x   ♢ x x x x   ♣ J x x

15. ♠ x x x x   ♡ x x   ♢ x x x   ♣ x x x x

ANSWERS

14. *Pass.* As far as you are concerned, any suit will do. Let your partner take himself out in *his* best suit.

15. *Bid 1 Spade.* Your longest suit.

QUIZ

You are West. The bidding has gone:

South	West	North	East
1 Diamond	Double	Pass	1 Heart
Pass			

What are your rebids when you hold:

16. ♠ A J x   ♡ A Q x x   ♢ x x x   ♣ K Q x

17. ♠ A K Q x   ♡ A Q x x   ♢ x   ♣ K Q J x

18. ♠ A K Q J x x   ♡ None   ♢ x x x x   ♣ A K Q

ANSWERS

16. *Rebid 2 Hearts,* showing 16, 17, or 18 points. With less than 16 points, you would pass.

17. *Rebid 4 Hearts,* showing 22 or more points.

18. *Rebid 4 Spades,* showing 22 points or more. You have a suit of your own.

QUIZ

19. Your right-hand opponent opens with *4 Hearts*. What is your bid?

    ♠ A K Q   ♡ x x   ◇ K Q J x   ♣ A Q 10 x

20. In the following hand, you are South and hold:

    ♠ A K 10 x   ♡ A Q J   ◇ x x   ♣ A K J x

    The bidding has gone:

South	West	North	East
1 Club	1 Diamond	Pass	Pass

    What is your bid?

ANSWERS

19. *Bid 4 No Trump*. This is a super duper *Take-Out Double*. Your partner must name his best suit.

20. *Double*. This is a *Take-Out Double*. You have 23 points and all you need to know in order to try for a game is your partner's best suit.

CHAPTER XI

Playing the Hand

Playing the hand is the part of bridge that you can learn by trial and error. For this reason I feel there are more "expert" players than "expert" bidders. For many years, I was teaching my bridge students how to reach their proper contracts, but they weren't making their bids. I then decided that I must simplify the subject of playing the hand as I had done the subject of bidding. Since I was never willing to spend the time at the bridge table, in order to learn by trial and error and, I hope, my students won't either, I had to come up with a system of how to "think" the play of the hand; how to develop thought patterns.

First, as the Declarer, you must tell yourself, "I must take every trick in the deck." How many tricks in the deck are there?—thirteen; right? How many cards do you have in your hand? Thirteen. If every card in your hand is a winner—that is, a trick-taker, wouldn't you then take all thirteen tricks?

Let's assume you are playing a Spade contract and have the following hand:

♠ A K Q J 10 9   ♡ A K Q   ◇ A K Q   ♣ A

How many of these thirteen cards are losers? Obviously, if you take the opponents' trumps (Spades) away from them so they can't trump your good tricks, you will take all thirteen tricks; right? You don't even need help from the Dummy hand, especially if your contract is in No Trump, which would be best. Note that I didn't say how many

Spades you and Partner had to bid. I never discuss with my students the number of tricks they are to take in order to make their bid, but to "think" taking every trick they can.

Suppose, however, instead of the above hand, you have the following (playing a Spade contract):

♠ A K Q J 10 9   ♡ 4 3 2   ♢ A K Q   ♣ A

How many losers do you have? There are three Heart losers; right? Now you will have to figure out some way to avoid losing these three tricks. One way is with *high cards*; the other way is by *trumping*. Where do you look for help in eliminating the three Heart losers? In the Dummy's hand. After you have seen the danger of losing these three tricks, examine the Dummy and see what help is available.

Dummy has:

♠ 8 7   ♡ A K Q   ♢ 6 4 3 2   ♣ 6 4 3 2

With the above cards in the Dummy, you can play the three losing Hearts on the three *high cards*. Suppose the opponents lead a small Diamond. You would win the Diamond trick, draw the trumps by playing Spades until all thirteen Spades have been accounted for, and then play the rest of your *high-card* tricks. Thus you have taken all thirteen tricks.

Suppose, however, Dummy's hand is:

♠ 6 5 2   ♡ None   ♢ 7 6 5 3 2   ♣ 10 9 7 3 2

Can you still take thirteen tricks? Can you find a way to avoid losing the three Heart tricks? You don't have the *high cards* anymore. The only two ways to take tricks are with *high cards* and *trumps*. Can you find a way to run out of Hearts in the Dummy; and, if so, do you have three trumps with which to trump the three losing Hearts? Yes; you are already void in Hearts. If the opponents lead a Diamond, take the trick with the Ace, trump the three small Hearts, *draw* the trumps from the opponents' hands, and then play your *high-card* tricks.

Suppose this is Dummy's hand:

♠ 9 8 7 6 2   ♡ 8 7 6   ♢ None   ♣ 7 6 4 3 2

[123]

You still face the same three Heart losers; what now? There are no *high cards* on which you can throw these losers. You are not out of Hearts, so you can't *trump* these three Heart losers. What if you throw Dummy's three small Hearts on the Ace, King, and Queen of Diamonds, trump the three losing Hearts, draw the rest of the trumps, and then play your remaining *high-card* tricks? This will work; but if the opponents happen to lead Hearts, you'll lose the three Hearts tricks right away, before you have the chance to do anything about it.

Now let's assume you are playing the following hand at another Spade contract:

Dummy's hand:

♠ 7 6 5 2   ♡ A Q 3   ♢ 9 6 3   ♣ 5 4 3

Declarer's hand:

♠ A K Q J 9 4   ♡ 8 4   ♢ A K Q   ♣ A K

How many losers are there in the Declarer's hand? No losing Spades, two losing Hearts, no losing Diamonds, and no losing Clubs. Now look at the Dummy. Does Dummy have the A K of Hearts on which to dispose of the two losers in that suit? No; but perhaps you can figure a way to make the A Q perform as if they were the A K. Let's pretend you can place the missing King in either your left-hand opponent's possession or your right-hand opponent's. Would it make any difference? Think! Let's place it with your left-hand opponent and see what happens. If you play the Ace of Hearts first and then the Queen, naturally your opponent will capture your Queen with his King. What if you play your 8 of Hearts first, playing it up to the Dummy's hand; what would happen? If your left-hand opponent plays a low card, you will play the Queen from Dummy. Does this win the trick? Yes! Now you will play the Ace and both of your small cards have been disposed of. You may argue, "But if the King had been in the hand of the right-hand opponent, my Queen would have been lost." You are right; but half the time we figure it will be at your left. This is called a *finesse* and can be used anytime you have a suit that has a "hole" in it; meaning that one of the honors is missing.

[124]

Assume the opening lead in this hand is a Diamond: Take the first trick with the Ace of Diamonds, *draw* the trumps from the opponents, *finesse* the A Q, and then take your *high-card* Club tricks and the rest of your *high-card* Diamond tricks.

In the next hand, you are the Declarer playing a Heart contract:

Dummy's hand

♠ A 9 7 3   ♡ K Q 6 2   ◇ J 8 4   ♣ 8 4

Declarer's hand

♠ 5   ♡ A J 10 7 3   ◇ 9 5   ♣ A K 7 5 2

How many losers are there in the Declarer's hand? One in Spades, four in Hearts, two in Diamonds, and three in Clubs. Ten losers out of a possible thirteen winners. Is there anything the Declarer can do with the help of Dummy to avoid all these losers? Examine the Dummy's hand; take the losers one at a time—and *think!* What about the 5 of Spades? Dummy has the Ace, so this loser is saved. Since Dummy has plenty of Hearts, there are no problems with this suit. The two Diamond losers cannot be avoided. The Clubs, however, can be played in such a way that at least some of the small cards will be able to take tricks. This we call *establishing a side suit* or setting up *long cards*. (Often done in playing No Trump contracts.)

Let's assume the opponent leads a Diamond. You will then lose two Diamonds, trump the third one if that suit is continued, *draw* the trumps until all are accounted for, and lead the Ace and King of Clubs. If the opponents have followed suit each time in Clubs, this means that eight Clubs have been played, and three are left in the Declarer's hand, leaving the opponents with two. Play a small Club and trump in the Dummy. If the two outstanding Clubs fall on this trick your last two Clubs (*long cards*) are trick-takers.

Study the following hand. You are the Declarer, playing a Heart contract:

Dummy's hand

♠ A 8 7 6 3   ♡ 10 9 8 4   ◇ 3   ♣ 8 7 3

♠ 4   ♡ A K Q J   ◇ A 9 8 5 4   ♣ A 6 5

The opening lead is the Queen of Spades. How many losing tricks does the Declarer have? One in Spades, none in Hearts, four in Diamonds, and two in Clubs. Seven losers out of thirteen possible winners. Can Dummy's hand help to do away with any of the losers? Dummy's Ace of Spades gets rid of one Spade loser. Can you trump four Diamond losers? Yes! Should you draw the opponents' trumps first? If you do, you will deprive yourself of the four Hearts in the Dummy which you need in order to trump the four losing Diamonds. Obviously, then, you *won't* ever *draw* trumps in this hand. You will take the Queen of Spades with the Ace of Spades, play the 3 of Diamonds from Dummy's hand, overtaking it with the Ace in your own hand, trump the 4 of Diamonds in Dummy, get back again to your hand with the Ace of Clubs, trump another Diamond, return to your hand by trumping a small Spade, trump the 8 of Diamonds, get back to your hand by trumping another Spade, and trump your last loser in Diamonds. This is called *cross-ruffing* or *cross-trumping*. I must point out here that you did not trump Spades because they were losers, but because the Spades were the means of getting back to Declarer's hand each time so that the losing Diamonds could be trumped.

Let's play another hand. You are the Declarer in a Diamond contract.

Dummy's hand

♠ K Q 7 3 2   ♡ A K 9   ◇ Q J 10 4   ♣ 8

Declarer's hand

♠ 5   ♡ 5 4   ◇ A K 9 8 3   ♣ A J 6 5 4

The opening lead is the 7 of Diamonds.

If the opponent had not led a Diamond you would have been able to *cross-ruff* this hand. You must realize that the opponent listened to the bidding and recognized that a trump lead would be a good defensive play, and when you play your King of Spades it will be captured with the Ace and opponents will continue leading trumps. Therefore you must change your strategy. Count your losers, as before. You can see at once that the Dummy's hand has fewer losers than the Declarer's. Wouldn't it be easier to count the losers in Dummy's hand and use the Declarer's hand to get rid of those losers? Since you have Diamonds (trumps) in Declarer's hand, couldn't you set up Dummy's *long cards* in Spades? This is called a *Dummy reversal*. It simply means using the Dummy as a base for counting losing cards because it is easier than using the Declarer's hand.

You, as Declarer, are playing a contract in Hearts.

Dummy's hand

♠ K 7 6   ♡ 5 4 3   ◇ A K Q 5   ♣ 8 5 3

Declarer's hand

♠ 4   ♡ A J 10 9 8 7 6 2   ◇ None   ♣ K 6 4 2

The opening lead is the Queen of Spades, which appears to be the top of an honor sequence (Q J 10).

You have one Spade loser. If the two Hearts, the King and Queen, are in the same hand, you will lose one. If they are divided between your opponents, you will not lose a Heart trick. There are no Diamond losers because your hand is void in that suit. And you have four possible Club losers.

Looking at Dummy's hand! There are three *high-card* Diamond tricks there; right? If Diamonds had been led originally, you could have thrown three of your losing Clubs on the three high Diamonds and most of your problems would have been solved.

Since the opponents aren't usually so obliging, you must find some way to get over to the Dummy in order to make use of the high Diamonds.

You may have the urge to put Dummy's King of Spades on the opening lead of the Queen, especially if you have friends who "always cover an honor with an honor." Not so! Stop and think. Your right-hand opponent must have the Ace of Spades. Why? Because the left-hand

[127]

opponent would hardly have led the suit from the A Q. Suits that have holes in them are *waiting suits*, not *leading suits*.

So if you play the Dummy's King of Spades, your right-hand opponent will grab it with his Ace; and if he has the Queen of Clubs (as in this hand he did) he may lead it, forcing you to put on your King, and your left-hand opponent will have a field day with your Club losers.

To avoid such a disaster, play the 6 of Spades and trump the second round of Spades in your own hand. Now, if you were thinking carefully when you trumped the Spade, you can lay down your Ace of trumps (the King and Queen fall), get to the Dummy, and throw off your Club losers on the Diamonds. If, however, you trumped the Spade with the 2 of Hearts, you can't do it. The trick had to be trumped with the 6-spot and now you have the 2 of Hearts, which can be taken in Dummy by the 3, 4, or 5. Throw off your losing Clubs and win the rest of the tricks.

By now you have seen that sometimes you *draw trumps* immediately; sometimes you *delay drawing trumps;* and sometimes you deliberately *avoid drawing trumps*.

Each of these situations is determined by first counting your losers in one hand (the stronger) and using the other hand as a means of disposing of the losers. If you have determined that it won't be necessary to trump a loser, then *draw trumps* immediately. Then take your remaining *high-card* tricks.

If you find, however, that you have a long suit in your hand which can be trumped and another suit in the other hand that you need to trump for transportation purposes, then *don't draw trumps at all!*

THE NAME OF THE PLAYING GAME IS TAKING TRICKS. THINK! LEARN TO COUNT YOUR LOSERS IN EACH HAND SO THAT YOU CAN ELIMINATE THEM AS LOSERS. REMEMBER, THERE ARE ONLY TWO WAYS TO TAKE TRICKS—WITH *High Cards* AND BY *Trumping*.

IF YOU ARE PLAYING A NO TRUMP CONTRACT, THERE IS ONLY ONE WAY TO TAKE ALL THE TRICKS—WITH *High Cards*. LONG SUITS MUST BE SET UP WHILE YOU STILL HAVE ENTRIES IN THE OTHER SUITS.

In the following hand you are the Declarer, playing a No Trump contract.

Dummy's hand

♠ 6 2   ♡ K Q 4   ◇ J 7 4 2   ♣ K 8 4 3

Declarer's hand

♠ A 8 7   ♡ A 9 6 2   ◇ K Q 8 3   ♣ A 6

The opening lead is the King of Spades.

There aren't too many absolutes in bridge, but one thing you can be pretty sure of: the opponents are going to attack your weakest suit. This hand is no exception. Remember, the only way you can win tricks in a No Trump contract is with *high cards*! The highest remaining card in a suit takes the trick. Therefore you must set up *long cards*.

In No Trump contracts you can count your sure winners and then figure out how you might establish *long cards* that will enable you to take the tricks needed to fulfill the contract. *And you must set up* these *long cards* while you still have entries in the other suits.

How many winners do you have? One in Spades; maybe four in Hearts (depending on the distribution); at least two Diamonds (after you force out the opponents' Ace); and two in Clubs. In any case, you must force out the Ace of Diamonds and this must be done while you are still in control of the other suits.

When you have taken your only trick in Spades with the Ace, you will want to play the King of Diamonds in order to set up that suit. Stop and think! When the Ace of Diamonds is played, won't the opponents persist with the Spades? Obviously they have a raft of them, since you have so few. But they will not be able to lead back Spades if the opponent who grabs a trick with the Ace of Diamonds has no Spades to lead.

Let's hope the opponent with the Ace of Diamonds doesn't have a five-card Spade suit. If such is the case, you can guard against it by holding up your Ace of Spades until the third round; then the opponent with the Ace of Diamonds may be out of Spades and will be compelled to lead some other suit. Had you won the first Spade trick with the Ace, the opponent with the highest Diamond would still have a Spade to return to his partner. But by means of the *hold-up*, so called, you can claim nine tricks.

Here is another No Trump hand:

Dummy's hand

♠ K 5 4   ♡ 8 7 2   ◇ A 10 5 4 2   ♣ K 7

Declarer's hand

♠ A 9 8 3   ♡ A 9 6 4   ◇ K Q   ♣ A 8 3

The opening lead is the Queen of Clubs, probably the top card of an honor sequence.

This is one time the opponents did not lead the suit in which you had only one stopper—Hearts. But you must think before you play or you may land in trouble. The combined hands count to eight tricks, and nine are needed to fulfill a 3 No Trump contract. Whenever you are in a No Trump effort you must look for a long suit to set up. Examine your Diamond holding. Your hope is to win five tricks in that suit. The opponents do not cooperate, however. The suit is divided so that four cards—J 9 6 3—are in one hand. When you discover that the Jack will not fall, lead the suit again; give up the trick to the Jack. Now, when the return lead comes back to you, the *long card*—the little deuce of Diamonds—becomes your ninth trick.

See what would have happened if you had taken the first Spade trick with the Dummy's King. You would have used up a valuable entry to Dummy's hand and could never have got back to the Dummy to score that important *long* Diamond. Review this maneuver; it occurs often, and if you master it you cannot fail.

Your first trick should be taken in Declarer's hand with the Ace of Spades. Now play the King and Queen of Diamonds; then a small Club, taken by the Dummy's King. Next, play the Ace of Diamonds— this is when you find out that the Jack doesn't fall. Continue with the Diamonds; let the Jack win. Now, it makes no difference what the opponents do; you still have the King of Spades left in Dummy so that you can play the *long* Diamond.

In this way you are playing expert bridge, because you have learned to *think*—to count your possible winners. It isn't always easy. After a hard day's work, thinking is sometimes a little too strenuous. In any case, enjoy the game. Remember—the scientific goal of bridge is winning tricks; the social goal is winning friends. Best of luck to you at both!

SIGNALING

Talk to Partner with the cards you play.

When defending a contract, you will want to give Partner some information about your hand. When he gets in the lead you'll want him to lead the suits that will enable you to take tricks.

Telling him this is very simple. Any time you play the 2-, 3-, 4-, or 5-spot you are telling him that this is not the suit you want him to lead. If you put the 6-, 7-, 8-, or 9-spot on the trick, you are informing him to *continue* to lead that suit.

It isn't always easy to signal.

Suppose Partner leads the Ace of Spades and you have the King and the 3- and 2-spot of Spades, you can signal to partner that you want him to lead the suit again so that you can take the next trick with your King—that is, if he is a thinking partner. The best you can do is signal with the 3-spot; right? Well, Partner can see his cards and also see the Dummy's cards, and by now the Declarer has played to the trick. If the Declarer had had the 2-spot, don't you think this would have been the logical card to play? And if he didn't play it, won't a thinking partner realize it must be in your hand? Therefore the 3-spot must not have been the lowest card you had, and it was a signal card.

Sometimes your biggest problem at the bridge table is that your opponents are also thinking. Suppose the Declarer had the 2-spot but wanted the Spade suit continued—couldn't he hold on to it and throw a higher card on the trick?

SUIT PREFERENCE SIGNALS

The *suit preference signal* can be very helpful in both defensive positions. Suppose you have the opening lead against a Spade contract and have led the King of Hearts from the A K x. The following Dummy hand is put down:

♠ J 10 9 7   ♡ x   ◇ K Q J x   ♣ K Q J x

The small Heart is played from the Dummy hand and your partner plays the 9 of Hearts. Isn't it obvious that Partner doesn't want the Heart continued since Dummy will surely trump? He isn't asking for a trump lead so what does he want? The other two suits are Diamonds and Clubs. The *high card* is asking for the *higher-ranking suit* which is Diamonds. A *low card* would be asking for a Club return.

In the other defensive position, suppose your partner has led the King of Spades. The Q x x x is in the Dummy and you have a doubleton, the 9- and 2-spots. You play high and then low on partner's King and Ace. He knows that you are now planning to trump the third Spade. If he has an immediate re-entry to his hand he can lead a fourth Spade and you will be able to trump again.

If Hearts are trumps then the two outside suits are Diamonds and Clubs. If he is able to re-enter his hand with Diamonds he will lead a high card for you to trump; if it is Clubs he will lead low.

The *suit preference* signal takes a *great deal of the guess out of the defense.*

CHAPTER XII

Leads

One of the most common phrases heard at the bridge table among beginner players is: "I never know what to lead." The lead requires about as much thought and concentration as any part of the bridge game.

Every suit in your hand is either a "leading suit" or a "waiting suit."

Before you make your decision as to your lead, there are a number of questions that you should ask yourself:

1. Am I making the *Opening Lead,* or am I leading to a later trick?

2. Is this a suit bid or a No Trump bid?

3. How did the bidding go? Who bid the Spades, Hearts, Diamonds, or Clubs? Was it my team or my opponents' team?

4. Will this lead force a high card out of my partner's hand? If so, will it set up a future trick for me?

5. Do I have a suit that my partner is probably void in, and if so, does he have any trumps left with which to trump?

6. Is my opponent (the *Declarer*) out of this suit in both his hand and the *Dummy* hand? If so, I will not want to lead it because he can trump it in one hand and throw off a losing card in the other hand.

7. If I lead this card, will it set up a future trick for my team or will it help my opponents set up their tricks?

(*Even though you have previously lost a trick in a suit, when it is your turn to lead again, unless you have a better lead, continue leading the same suit.*)

[133]

YOUR PLAN OF ATTACK AS THE OPENING LEADER

When it is your turn to be the *Opening Leader*, you will want to do one of the following:

1. Take your tricks immediately.

2. Set up tricks to take later.

3. Wait for suits to be led to you. (Don't lead suits with holes in them.)

4. Lead trumps.

5. Lead short suits.

6. Lead the suit that your partner bid.

7. Lead in the dark.

1. *Take your tricks immediately.* If you have the A K Q, A K x, or A K, you may want to take them immediately. If you have the A K Q, lead the King and then the Queen. This will tell your partner that you have the Ace also. If you have the A K x, lead the King and then the Ace. This will tell your partner that you have the A K and not the Queen. If, however, you have just the A K alone, lead the Ace and then the King. Anytime you lead a higher card and then a lower card, it is a *Signal* to your partner that you have only two cards in that suit. Your partner will know that you can trump the next card led in that suit.

2. *Set up tricks to take later.* When you lead the top of a sequence of *Honors*, you are setting up tricks to take later. If you have K Q J, lead the King which will lose to the Ace, but your Q J will set up to take tricks later. With the Q J 10, you may lose the Q J to the A K, but you will set up the 10-spot.

3. *Wait for suits to be led to you.*

    a. *Don't* lead suits that have only one high card; i.e., A x x x, K x x x, Q x x x, etc. *Wait* for this suits to be led to you.

If you are forced to lead one of these suits because it is the least undesirable lead in your hand, then you should lead the Ace rather than leading from it. However, if the suit is headed by the King or Queen you should lead the fourth card down.

b. *Don't* lead from *Tenaces.* (A *Tenace* is a three- or four-card sequence of touching honors with one of the *middle* honors missing, or, as one of my students said, "Oh, a suit that has a hole in it," i.e., A Q J, K J 10, etc. *Wait* for these suits to be led to you because if you do, your chances are good that you will make them perform as if they were a sequence.

4. *Lead trumps.* One of the most famous phrases in bridge is, "When in doubt lead trumps." This should be changed to: "Never lead trumps when there is a doubt." There is one definite reason for leading trumps: "When you want the opponents to spend two trumps at one time." If you think your opponents are planning on using their trumps for *cross-ruffing* where they can make two trumps (one in each hand) take two tricks instead of one, you should lead trumps. If your opponents who are *Declarer* and the *Dummy* have four trumps in each hand and they are forced to play trumps or if they lead trumps, they will take only four tricks. Right? But, if they have short suits in both hands, they can *cross-trump*, and it's possible to take eight tricks; so every time you lead a trump you have cut their trick-taking values down by one.

As the *Opening Leader* how can you know whether your opponents will have such a thought as this in mind? Let's examine the bidding:

South	West	North	East
1 Diamond	Pass	1 Spade	Pass
2 Hearts	Pass	4 Hearts	Pass

South opened the bidding with *1 Diamond* and then bid Hearts. What does this tell you? That he has five Diamonds and four Hearts. How do you know this? Because if he had had five diamonds and five Hearts or four of each he would have bid the Heart suit first. Right? He has four cards left so he either has two doubletons, a singleton, or

[135]

a void, and he may want to use his trumps for *cross-trumping* these short suits.

North definitely has four Hearts because he couldn't have jumped to *4 Hearts* without four of Partner's suit, since South indicated he had a four-card suit. North either had a four- or five-card Spade suit. With this eight- or nine-card holding he must have at least one doubleton and possibly a singleton or a void, so the *Declarer* may want to use North's trumps for *cross-trumping*, too.

5. *Lead short suits*. A short suit may be a good lead if you have trumps to spare and if you feel sure that your partner can get in the lead and lead the suit to you for you to trump before the opponents have drawn your trumps. If you have K x, Q x x, J x x x, then you do not have trumps to spare because if you use a card for trumping, you will unguard your honor and probably lose your honor card. If you have A x or A x x x or any number of small cards, you have trumps to spare.

6. *Lead the suit that your partner bid*. Many players feel that you should always lead the highest card in the suit that your partner has bid. You may do this if you have:

a. Only two cards; i.e., A x, K x, Q x, J x, etc.

b. The top of a three-card worthless suit.

c. The top of a sequence.

Otherwise lead the fourth card down so that your partner can count your cards.

If you have three cards to an honor, lead the low card and not the honor. Wait with the honor, hoping to catch your opponent's high card with it.

7. *Lead in the dark*. Quite often you will have hands that do not produce an attractive *Opening Lead*. When this happens, there are a couple of leads that you may use as a last resort.

a. *Lead from the top of nothing;* i.e., 9 8 7, 8 7 6, 7 3 2, etc.

b. Lead the fourth card down from a four- or five-card suit headed by the King, Queen, or Jack.

Note: Have you noticed that if your partner leads a high spot card, you will assume that he led from the "top of nothing"; and if he leads a small spot card, that he has an honor left in his hand.

OPENING LEADS AT NO TRUMP

In playing No Trump, you must learn how to take tricks with small cards. So, often, you will have to lose a few tricks in order to take a few. This is called "setting up" tricks. You must also have a "side suit trick" in order to get back into your hand to use the "long-card tricks."

EXAMPLES

♠ K Q J 10 x x x x   ♡ x x   ◇ x x   ♣ x

This hand should set up long-card tricks almost immediately, but how can you return to your hand and use them? Don't lead Spades at No Trump.

♠ K Q J 10 x x x x   ♡ A x   ◇ x x   ♣ x

After the first lead when you lose your King of Spades to the Ace, the other cards are set up; and the first time Hearts are led, you have returned to your hand to take all of your *long-card* tricks. Lead at No Trump.

EXAMPLE

♠ A x   ♡ A Q x x x   ◇ x x x   ♣ J x x

You have to make the opening lead at a *3 No Trump* contract. In a suit bid you would not lead the Heart suit; you would wait for it to be led to you because if you lead it, you will probably take only the Ace. If led to you, you may take the A Q, but after that the small cards will probably be trumped. In No Trump, however, you will want to lead the fourth card down from the top of this suit and deliberately lose a trick now but probably set up some *long-card* tricks later.

Remember: When playing a No Trump hand, whether you are the *Declarer* or the *Defender*, you should be willing to take a few losses in order to take more tricks with small cards later. If you have to have losers, you must take these losers while you still have high cards in side suits so that you can return to your hand and take your "set up" tricks.

THE RULE OF 11

When the Opening Lead is "the fourth down from the longest and strongest suit" (a common lead at No Trump), the *leader's partner and the Declarer* can count the number of cards in each other's hand that are higher than the card which was led, by using the *Rule of 11*. The spot on the led card is subtracted from 11. This will give the number of cards in the other *three hands* that are higher than the card led.

EXAMPLE

As South, *the Declarer*, you have the following cards in Spades: J 8 7.

North, *the dummy*, has in Spades: K 9 2.

West's opening lead is the 6 of Spades.

Six subtracted from 11 is 5. *Declarer* now recognizes that the 9-spot in Dummy will take the trick because, since he has three cards and the Dummy has two higher than the 5, East cannot cover the 9.

CHAPTER XIII

Free Responses

(OR FREE BIDS)

Recently one of my beginner students came to class very excited over her first bridge party. There was only one problem: "East and West wouldn't pass."

This is a problem in almost every bridge hand. You have opponents who want to get into the game, too. I have felt, however, that a beginner should be able to fully understand *Bidding*, *Responding* and *Rebidding* before we complicate things by trying to explain a *Free Bid*. Now that you have learned the important basics of bridge, I feel that you are ready for this complicated subject.

A *Free Bid* or a *Free Response* is a response given after the opponent, sitting to your right, has put in an *Overcall*. (In this respect we do not consider a *Take-Out Double* as an *Overcall*. You have already learned how to respond after a *Take-Out Double*.)

I have tried to simplify the formula for the *Free Response* so that you won't have to do so much memory work.

As you recall, a *raise in your partner's suit*, a response of *1 No Trump*, or a *1 over 1* or *2 over 1* indicates at least 6 points. Right? If you have a Primary hand with 6, 7, 8 or 9 points, you do one of the above. Well, now that the opponents have put in an *Overcall* if you make one of the above bids, you are indicating an Intermediate hand with 10, 11 or 12 points. (Your common sense will tell you that when you make a free response in No Trump the opponents' suit should be stopped.)

[139]

With a Primary hand you just pass. That's all there is to it. Bid all other responses just as if your opponents had passed.

You may be asking: "Why does it matter whether the opponents have put in a bid or not?" When you respond to your partner's opening bid with a 6- or 7-point hand, you are doing so just to enable your partner to *bid again* if he has a big hand. Since the opponents have *Overcalled*, doesn't he have that chance to bid again? Yes. So if you respond now you show at least 10 points.

CHAPTER XIV

Scoring

The ultimate goal in bridge is *scoring points*. You will find the scoring chart summarized at the end of this chapter, but please do not memorize it. You have too many other things to remember. Most scoring pads have the score chart on them, so use them until you are more familiar with scoring. This chapter is designed to get you acquainted with scoring terms.

THE SCORING PAD

On the scoring pad a line is drawn *across* the center of the pad to separate the *game points* from *all* other points. A line is drawn *down* the center of the pad to separate the opponents' scores. The *score keeper* will call his team "we" and his opponents' team "they." Points can be scored in the following ways:

1. By making games.

2. By making overtricks.

3. By making slams.

4. By making rubbers.

5. By having Honor Points.

6. By setting the *Declarer* (in the defensive play).

GAME

A *Game* is 100 *scoring points*. These points can be made by one bid such as:

4 Spades or Hearts—30 points each equals 120 points.

5 Diamonds or Clubs—20 points each equals 100 points.

3 No Trump—40 points for the first trick; 30 points for each of two additional tricks equals 100 points.

or it may take several bids to make 100 *scoring points*. Only the amount bid is added to the *game points* which is put below the line. *All other points are put above the line.*

OVERTRICKS

An *Overtrick* is just what it implies. If you bid *2 Spades* and make *4 Spades*, you have made two tricks over your bid. The bid of *2 Spades* (60 points) is put below the line, or in the space provided for the game score, and the 2 *Overtricks* (60 points) are put above the line.

RUBBERS

A *Rubber* is two out of three games. If one *Team* makes two games in a row, this is a 700-point *Rubber*. If three games have to be played it is a 500-point *Rubber*. (These points are put *above* the line.)

VULNERABILITY

When either team has made a game, it is *Vulnerable*. When a team is *Vulnerable*, the score points will change in several situations. A *Vulnerable* team will want to bid with more caution because if they get "set," their opponents will make more points. (See scoring chart.)

SLAMS

Little Slam. If the partnership is not vulnerable, it will get 500 bonus points put above the line for bidding and making the Little

Slam. If it is vulnerable, it will get 750 extra bonus points put above the line for making the Little Slam.

Grand Slam. If the partnership is not vulnerable, it will get 1000 bonus points put above the line for bidding and making the Grand Slam. If it *is* vulnerable, it will get 1500 bonus points put above the line for bidding and making the Grand Slam.

HONOR POINTS

If *Declarer* has *All* of the five honors (A K Q J 10) in his trump suit, in his hand or Dummy's, he receives 150 *Honor Points*, above the line. If he has any four of the five honors in one hand, he receives 100 *Honor Points*, above the line. If *Declarer* is playing a No Trump contract and has all 4 *Aces* in one hand, this will give him 150 *Honor Points*.

SETTING THE DECLARER
(DEFENSIVE SCORE)

The only way the *Defenders* can score in Bridge is by setting the opponents. So for this reason it is very important to learn how to play a good defensive game. So many players feel that unless they get the bid the fun is over until the next hand is dealt. Bridge can be just as interesting for the defenders as for the declarer. It requires as much if not more skill in playing the hand. If the *Declarer* gets set (does not make his bid contract), then the opponents make the score. It is put above the line. If the *Declarer's* team is not vulnerable, the defenders will get 50 points for each set trick. If vulnerable the defenders will receive 100 points for each set trick.

DOUBLE AND REDOUBLE

If the *Defender* has reason to believe the *Declarer* will not make his bid, he will say *Double*. It simply means that the final score will be doubled. (See scoring chart.)

If the *Declarer*, after he has been *doubled*, feels that he *can* make his bid, he will say *Redouble*. The final score will be doubled and redoubled. This score depends on the number of tricks the *Declarer* failed to take in order to make his contract. The final score will also depend on whether the *Declarer* is vulnerable or not vulnerable (See scoring chart.)

SCORING CHART SUMMARIZED

GAME REQUIREMENTS AND TRICK VALUES

Game Requires ....100 points
No Trump   1st trick .... 40 points
　　　　　　　All subsequent tricks .... 30 points
Spades and Hearts, each .... 30 points
Diamonds and Clubs, each .... 20 points

HONOR PREMIUMS

4 of the possible 5 honors in one hand 100
5 of the possible 5 honors in one hand 150
4 Aces (No Trump) in one hand 150

CONTRACT AND EXTRA TRICK PREMIUMS

Extra Tricks ....Same as game value of trick
　　Doubled—Not Vulnerable 100
　　Doubled—Vulnerable 200
　　For fulfilling contract doubled or redoubled 50

SLAM PREMIUMS

Small Slam—Not Vulnerable 500
　　Vulnerable 750
Grand Slam—Not Vulnerable 1000
　　Vulnerable 1500
　　No Premium for Unbid Slams.
　　Doubling does not affect Slam Bonus.

RUBBER PREMIUMS

3-Game Rubber 500
2-Game Rubber 700
Unfinished Rubber—1 game 300
If one side has a part score in an unfinished game 50

CUMULATIVE UNDERTRICK PENALTIES—TOTAL

Description	Not Vulnerable		Vulnerable	
	Undoubled	Doubled	Undoubled	Doubled
Set 1 Trick	50	100	100	200
Set 2 Tricks	100	300	200	500
Set 3 Tricks	150	500	300	800
Set 4 Tricks	200	700	400	1100
Set 5 Tricks	250	900	500	1400
Set 6 Tricks	300	1100	600	1700

Redoubling Doubles the Value of Doubled Contracts.

CHAPTER XV

Bridge Laws

I am substituting Mr. Hughes' "Call the Director" for my chapter on Bridge Laws in previous editions. Since his booklet is strictly for Duplicate Bridge, it does not include the Redeal, the No Redeal, and the Dummy's Rights. For this reason I am prefacing his "Call the Director" with these three subjects. All laws in "Call the Director" will apply to the rubber bridge games.

REDEAL

There shall be a redeal if a card is exposed during the deal or if one player has too many cards and another player has too few. Many times this will not be discovered until the last trick is to be played. If this happens, there is still a *Redeal*, and the same player who dealt the hand must deal again.

NO REDEAL

There will be *No Redeal* if one hand has a missing card and it is *found*. The lost card goes to the deficient hand. However, if any other player sees the card it must be considered an exposed card. It must be turned face up on the table and played the first time that suit is played or at the first opportunity to discard or trump. If the deficient hand is discovered later in the play and the card is found, there is still *No Redeal*. If the player did not follow suit, however, he shall be subject to a *Revoke penalty*.

DUMMY'S RIGHTS

If the *Dummy* has not seen a card in any of the other three hands his rights are as follows:

1. He may get or give information on any bridge law.

2. He may call attention to any *Revoke*.

3. He may ask his partner, who is the *Declarer*, if he is out of a suit when he has just discarded.

4. He may warn the *Declarer* against leading from the wrong hand if it is obvious that he is about to do so.

5. He may draw attention to any irregularity.

"CALL THE DIRECTOR"
By BOYD R. HUGHES
DUTY TO COUNT CARDS

It is the responsibility of each player to count his cards before seeing the face of them; failure to do so incurs a penalty of 1/10 of the possible match-points on the board. Cards should also be counted before returning them to the board. (9-122)

EXPOSED CARDS

(a) Declarer is never subject to penalty for exposure of a card, and no card of declarer ever becomes a penalty card.

(b) If declarer exposes his hand after an opening lead by the wrong defender, and before dummy has spread any part of his hand, dummy becomes declarer.

(c) If a defender faces a card on the table, or sees the face of a card belonging to his partner, it becomes a penalty card. (63-67)

EXPOSED CARD DURING AUCTION

(a) If an Ace, King, Queen or Jack or a lower card prematurely led, or more than one card, the owner's partner must pass when next it is his turn to call. Card must be left face up on the table; and if its owner becomes a defender, it is a penalty card.

(b) If a single card, lower than a Jack and not prematurely led, there is no penalty. (26)

IMPROPER CALLS

If a player calls before the penalty for an improper call by his right-hand opponent has been enforced, the auction proceeds as though it had been a proper call. (27)

CHANGING A CALL

If a player changes a call in any way and does so practically in the same breath, his last call stands. There is no penalty. (28)

CALL OUT OF ROTATION

A call out of rotation is void. The auction reverts to the player whose turn it was to call; and

(a) If a player has passed out of rotation before any player has bid or when it was the turn of the opponent on his right to call, the offender must pass when next it is his turn to call, then can bid as usual. (*Exception*—When the pass occurs after the left-hand opponent has bid, partner is barred for the duration of the auction.)

(b) Any call (other than a pass) requires the offender's partner to pass for the duration of the auction.

(c) If a player, whose turn it was to call, calls before attention has been drawn to a call out of rotation by his left-hand opponent, the auction proceeds as though that opponent had not called. (31-33)

CALL AFTER THE AUCTION IS CLOSED

A call made after the auction is closed is cancelled. If it was a pass by a defender, or any call by contractor, there is no penalty.

If it was a bid, double or redouble by a defender, declarer may require or forbid the other defender to lead a specified suit when first it is his turn to lead. (40)

PLAYED CARD

A card in any hand is played when named as the one a player proposes to play; but a player may change his designation if he does so practically in the same breath, *or if he designates a card which is not there.* (50)

DUMMY PLAYING WRONG CARD

If dummy places in the played position a card that declarer did not name, the card must be withdrawn if attention is called to it before a card has been led to the next trick, and a defender may withdraw a card played after the error but before attention was drawn to it. (45)

PLAYING BEFORE PENALTY HAS BEEN ENFORCED

If declarer plays from either hand before enforcing a lead or play penalty, he is deemed to waive the penalty. (60)

TWO CARDS PLAYED AT THE SAME TIME

If two cards are played by a defender at the same time, he can choose which to play; the other becomes a penalty card. (58)

INSPECTING TRICKS

Declarer or either defender may, until his side has led or played to the next trick, inspect the cards to a trick. (78)

LEAD OUT OF TURN (OPENING)

Declarer has three choices:

(1) He may accept the lead, the dummy is spread, then he plays, next his left-hand opponent and the dummy plays last.

(2) He may treat it as a penalty card and the proper leader may lead any card he chooses.

(3) He may prohibit the lead of that suit, in which case, the card is returned to offender's hand and does not become a penalty card. (55)

LEAD OUT OF TURN (SUBSEQUENT)

A lead out of turn may be treated as a correct lead. It must be so treated if the non-offending side plays a card before attention is drawn to the irregularity.

If declarer leads out of turn, the card led is replaced without penalty.

If declarer leads from the wrong hand, the card is replaced and he must lead the same suit, if he can, from the correct hand, and may play any proper card from the other; if the correct hand does not contain a card of the suit wrongly led, any card may be led.

If it was the declarer's turn to lead, declarer leads from the correct hand and the offender's card becomes a penalty card.

If it was the other defender's turn to lead,

(a) Declarer may forbid the lead of that suit, in which case the card is picked up.

(b) He may treat it as a penalty card and the proper player may lead any card he chooses. (55-57)

PREMATURE LEAD OR PLAY BY A DEFENDER

If a defender leads to the next trick before his partner has played to the current trick, or plays out of rotation before his partner has played, declarer may require the offender's partner to play:

(a) His highest card of the suit; or

(b) His lowest card of the suit; or

(c) A card of another specified suit. (54)

INSUFFICIENT BID

If a player makes an insufficient bid, he must substitute either a sufficient bid or a pass. (He cannot double.) If he substitutes—

(a) The lowest sufficient bid in the same denomination, there is no penalty.

(b) Any other bid (other than a pass), the offender's partner must pass for the duration of the auction.

(c) A pass, the offender's partner must pass for the duration of the auction; and if the offending side becomes the defenders, declarer may require or forbid the opening lead of a specified suit. (30)

DOUBLING PARTNER'S BID

The offender must substitute any proper call and his partner must pass for the duration of the auction. (37)

DECLARER CLAIMING OR CONCEDING TRICKS

If a declarer exposes his hand, claims or concedes one or more tricks:

(a) Declarer should place and leave his hand face up on the table and make an adequate statement of his intended line of play.

(b) He cannot change his stated line of play or take a finesse unless so stated.

(c) At any time after declarer's claim a defender may face his hand and suggest a play to his partner. (88)

REVOKE

A revoke must be corrected if attention is called to it before it becomes established; any player may call attention, including dummy.

There is no penalty for revoke at the twelfth trick and it never becomes established.

To correct a revoke, the card becomes a penalty card and any proper card may be played.

The non-offending side may withdraw any card it played after the revoke, but before attention was drawn to it.

A revoke is established when the offender or his partner plays to the next trick.

When a revoke is established, the revoke trick stands as played. It counts in transferring tricks as a trick won "after the revoke."

After play ceases, if the revoke has become established, two tricks are transferred to non-offending side if offenders have won two tricks after the revoke, including the revoke trick.

If only one trick is won after revoke, only one trick will be transferred. Tricks won before revoke cannot be transferred. (71-76)

[151]

REVIEWING THE AUCTION

A player may ask for a review of the auction when it is his turn to call or after the auction closes. (His request should be responded to only by an opponent.) After the opening lead, calls may not be reviewed. (Contract may be stated anytime.) (41-42)

LEARNING BRIDGE RULES IS A LUXURY TO A BRIDGE PLAYER. USING GOOD COMMON SENSE IS A NECESSITY.